The First Transition: Home to Pre-school

The First Transition: Home to Pre-school

A Report on the 'Transition from Home to Pre-school' Project

Peter Blatchford Sandra Battle Julia Mays

NFER-Nelson

Published by The NFER-Nelson Publishing Company Ltd,
Darville House, 2 Oxford Road East,
Windsor, Berks SL4 1DF

First Published 1982
© *NFER, 1982*
ISBN   0-7005-0493-1
Code   8090-02-1

Printed in Great Britain by
Biddles Ltd, Guildford, Surrey

Contents

List of Appendices

The following appendices can also be obtained on application:

> Entry into Nursery School and Class Questionnaire
> Entry into Playgroup Questionnaire
> Parent's Interview Schedule/Grid
> Child Adjustment Questionnaire
> Parent follow-up: interview guidelines

Requests for copies should be sent to:

> The National Foundation for Educational Research in
>   England and Wales
> The Mere
> Upton Park
> Slough
> Berks SL1 2DQ

Acknowledgments

The authors would like to thank the many nursery school, nursery class and playgroup staff, and parents, who took part in the survey. We express our special thanks to the staff, and children in the two nursery classes we studied in more depth. Their patience and good will made our visits pleasant occasions.

We would also like to express our gratitude to the following people for their helpful and perceptive comments on an earlier draft of the report: Shirley Cleave, Brian Goacher, Sandra Jowett and Clifford Morris. The team would also like to express their appreciation to Claire Creaser for her prompt and thorough statistical help. Finally, thanks are due to Beulah Matthews, Eva Forster, Sue Gibson and Muriel Bridge for their secretarial help.

Foreword

This report comes out during a very difficult time for nursery education. The deepening economic recession and government policies on public spending are causing many local authorities to review their existing service in the search for more economies. The anticipated expansion of nursery education pronounced in the government White Paper *Education: A Framework for Expansion* in 1972 is now a matter for the history books. The heady days following Plowden and the EPA studies – when great hopes were placed on nursery education as a tool of social change – have been replaced by a more defensive attitude. Few people now see much hope of Britain bringing the number of children entering nursery education into line with other countries in Europe.

Practitioners in the field could therefore be forgiven doubts about research into the pre-school field at a time when they are more concerned with conserving what currently exists. Yet, paradoxically, it is perhaps at such times that research can be most effective in suggesting ways existing resources and ideas might best be adapted to new circumstances. Certainly the continued coexistence of state aided and voluntary pre-school provision raises a number of issues concerning their respective contributions and what kind of dialogue is required between them. Issues are also raised by the growing reappraisal of the present divisive and uncoordinated provision in Britain, and the need to aid continuity between settings, for example from home to pre-school, and pre-school to primary school.

It was in this context that the National Foundation for Educational Research (NFER) instigated three research projects concerned with transition and continuity in the early years. The first, 'Continuity of Children's Experience in the years 3 to 8', funded by the DES, was designed to describe the experiences of children in different types of pre-school, and in primary school, in order to highlight points of continuity and discontinuity between the various stages (Cleave, Jowett and Bate, 1982).

Closely aligned to this project was another, 'Transition and Continuity in Early Education', funded by the Schools Council, which aimed to make practical use of the findings of the DES project by setting up liaison groups comprising personnel from pre-school and primary settings. These meetings involved parents, childminders and day care staff, as well as nursery, play-group and primary personnel.

The third project and the subject of the present report was funded by the NFER and entitled 'Transition from Home to Pre-school'. Whereas the first two projects were concerned with transition from pre-school to primary school, this was designed to study the first and prior transition from home to pre-school. As we shall see, the popular conception of the break from home to school taking place at five or so no longer holds, for the majority of under-fives will enter a pre-school setting of some kind. This project there-fore looked at the first link in a chain of transitions the child will pass through in his life. Together with the other two projects it was hoped to obtain a complete account of transition in the early years.

A number of different research methods – observational, interview and questionnaire – were used to address several questions concerning the first transition. Cutting across so many issues, as this project did, necessitated concern over the organization of the report. Our decision was to organize it in chronological fashion around the steps taken by children. Thus, after an introduction to the study (Chapter 1), and a general survey of nursery classes and schools and playgroups (Chapter 2), we present a discussion of interviews with parents prior to their child's entry (Chapter 3), an account of children's behaviour on entry (Chapter 4 and Chapter 5), a discussion of further interviews with parents several months after their child's entry (Chapter 6) and, finally, a summary of findings and conclusions (Chapter 7).

CHAPTER 1

Introduction

1. Background to the study

i. *Why investigate the transition from home to pre-school?*

A child's life in Britain is made up of a chain of transitions, taking him or her from one setting to another. By and large the pattern would be home to school, primary to secondary school and school to work. Each of these transitions has received attention from educational researchers and practitioners, with a view toward making transitions between stages in a child's life as smooth and productive as possible. The recommendations of the Plowden Committee (1967), for example, were influential in the setting up of middle schools to which children moved up from infant schools at the age of eight instead of the then usual age of seven. The Committee believed that the resulting extension of the first stage of education to three years would allow children time to firmly grasp the basics of reading.

The popular view would be that the first major transition is at the age of five years or so when children enter infant or first school. Attention has been paid toward easing the transition for children at this crucial time (Palmer, 1971; The Plowden Report, 1967; Renwick, 1978). Yet in a very real sense there is an earlier transition to which far less attention has been paid. This is the transition from home into pre-school settings such as nursery classes and schools, playgroups, day nurseries and childminders. Despite the generally held view that there is not enough provision for the under-fives, it is a fact, to be shown below, that the majority of them will at some point attend a pre-school of one kind or another, and that the majority of children will therefore go not straight from home to school but first from home to pre-school.

This study is about this very first type of transition; it investigates, amongst other things, the behaviour of children on entry, how staff approach entry and the views of parents.

It is an important time for all involved. For the child it is likely to be the first time he will have left, for any length of time, the relative familiarity and security of the home for a probably frightening environment at first with a different organization and personnel. Settings like nursery schools and classes, playgroups and day nurseries will in particular place different demands on the child, including those stemming from large numbers of peers, variety of play material and strange adults; and such settings are likely to be more impersonal than the home environment.

It is also an important time for the pre-school staff because they have responsibility for the child's first entry into a wider culture. This is most clearly seen in the case of nursery schools and classes where education in the formal sense begins, and where society therefore has a special interest in, and formal responsibility for, the child's time and experience. This is a serious responsibility, not least because first experiences may set up an enduring pattern that will structure the child's reactions to settings he will encounter later in his life.

The importance to parents of their child's entry into pre-school should not be underestimated. For many parents it will be the first time that they will be obliged to place the care of their child – at least partly – into the hands of another person. This must be threatening in some degree because it marks a significant turning point in their relationships with their child. But over and above this, parents' attitudes and views will obviously exert a powerful influence on their child's reactions to pre-school, for the child is likely even after entry to spend the bulk of his time at home.

Transition from home to pre-school therefore fundamentally involves three parties – children, pre-school and parents – and is important to all three. There has been, however, relatively little attention paid in the past to this first transition, either conceptually, in terms of a general understanding of the overall issues involved, or empirically, in terms of, for example, how children behave when they enter nursery, and what strategies are used or might be used to make the transition as productive and smooth as possible.

ii. *The concept of transition*

Several general considerations in the use and understanding of the term 'transition' in this study need to be mentioned. In the first place, though transition from home to pre-school can be seen to denote the single event of entry into pre-school, it is more usefully conceived as a complex process that subsumes a number of different events and points of view. Consideration of transition should not begin and end simply with a study of how children react to entry, but should also cover the situation prior to entry, in terms of the experiences of children in their home environment and the views of their parents, for these are important determinants of children's behaviour at pre-school and of the extent to which the families' needs are being met. Also relevant is the situation after entry in terms of children's continuing adjustment to pre-school and relations between staff and parents.

An assessment of how transition affects children is also best conceived not in one direction, i.e. from home to pre-school, but in terms of a continual and changing interplay of effects between the child's experiences in the pre-school and his home environment. It will be seen below how these considerations have structured the objectives of the research.

It is probably an arid enterprise to attempt a detailed formal definition of 'transition', but it is important to note that conceptions of transition are held, albeit implicitly, and that these do exert an influence on pre-school organization. For example there is a popular assumption that children are only ready for pre-school life at about three years of age. Historically this idea owes much to the work of John Bowlby (1965 (1953), 1971). In brief, Bowlby in a report for the World Health Organisation (1953), argued that a constant one-to-one relationship between the young child and his mother is essential for the child's normal social and intellectual development. The mother–infant relationship was credited later by Bowlby (1971) with a special instinctual basis in the survival of the human species. This view about the harmful effects of 'maternal deprivation' had a profound effect on pre-school facilities and care for the under-fives and has been one important factor in the widely held view that the child's early years are best spent in close proximity to his mother.

However, this view has come under attack from a number of directions (e.g. Casler, 1961; Clarke and Clarke, 1976; Rutter, 1972; Schaffer and Emerson, 1964). In an early criticism, Casler argued that much of the evidence for Bowlby's 'maternal deprivation' hypothesis came from studies of children brought up in residential institutions, often in rather clinical and unstimulating conditions, and that maternal deprivation was therefore confounded with other forms of deprivation, e.g. lack of social or even visual and physical stimulation, that might also affect children's development. Recent research has shown, moreover, that the child's relationship with people other than the mother may be underestimated by such a view. For example, it is becoming recognized that the young child's relations with other young children may have been previously undervalued and may in fact represent a rather different form of relationship with rather different functions to adult–infant relations (Blatchford, 1979; Lewis *et al.*, 1975). It is unlikely that parents, or even pre-school staff, will have studied Bowlby formally, but his views, nonetheless, have filtered through into everyday attitudes.

This is not the place to analyse Bowlby's theory in any depth – it is presented more in order to show that conceptions of transition do exist, however implicitly. The point to make is that a sound policy of pre-school provision depends on a clear and overt appraisal of transition and this does not seem to have been attempted. There is little doubt that provision in this case has come about in a piecemeal fashion.

iii. *Studying transition*

Apart from a general conceptualization of transition there is only a patchy account available from the research literature about a number of very real empirical issues affecting children, pre-school staff and parents. Such studies as do exist have tended to look exclusively at children's behaviour on entry (Baum, 1953; Murton, 1971; McGrew, 1972). Relevant as these studies are, they provide only a partial account in terms of the questions they asked and the breadth of their perspective.

It would be naïve to suppose that research can provide definitive answers to issues in this area, but there are sound reasons for using research techniques, and particularly observational methods, because of the systematic and hopefully objective description of behaviour that they can provide. Another contribution is of a more practical nature. In exploratory interviews with staff we discovered many ways in which they dealt with transition, some of which we believed were good examples of resourceful thinking. To document at least some of these achievements should be of benefit to others facing similar issues.

Before we move on to discuss the areas studied and research design it is first appropriate to give a brief overview of the extent of pre-school provision and the age at which children enter pre-schools in Britain, for this will enable us to put the present study into context.

iv. *Statistics on pre-school provision*

Anyone viewing the extent and type of pre-school provision in this country can be easily forgiven for finding it confused and uncoordinated. It has often been pointed out that this owes much to the fact that some forms of pre-school provision are under the auspices of the DES (nursery schools and classes, private nursery schools) whilst others come within the province of the DHSS (day and residential nurseries, playgroups, childminders). Apart from the differences in orientation that this division of responsibility necessarily encourages – a division, moreover, that owes nothing to the psychological development of the child but everything to administrative expediency – there is the added problem that different pre-schools have different philosophies, organization, resources, hours of attendance and ages of entry.

This makes the reliable collection and synthesis of statistics on provision very difficult. No attempt will be made here to review the statistics in depth and the interested reader is referred to the excellent summaries in Hughes *et al.* (1980); Tizard, Moss and Perry (1976) and van der Eyken (1977).

The different types of provision for under-fives can be divided into seven groups (Hughes *et al.*, 1980):

Nursery schools and classes - provided by local education authorities. Nursery schools are larger (on average 52 places as opposed to 25 places per school in nursery classes) and unlike nursery classes are not attached to primary schools. A minority of children stay the full school day in these two settings.

Reception classes - these take other under-fives in primary schools. Classes may contain older children as well. There are many 'rising fives' (children approaching five years of age) and attendance is predominantly for a full day.

Local authority day nurseries - provided by local authority social service departments for children defined as in special need (e.g. children with one parent, handicapped children, children with impoverished home environments). Most children attend full-time. The premises are separate buildings, the average number of places being 47.

Playgroups - provided by parent committees, local organizations, child-care charities, private proprietors and local authorities. Hours of attendance are predominantly part-time and children do not normally attend five sessions a week. (In one survey - Bone, 1977 - 68 per cent of children went to only one or two sessions a week.) A fee is charged, accommodation is usually in halls or other public buildings, and there are 27 places per playgroup on average.

Registered childminders - provided by individual minders in their own homes who must be registered with the local social service department and who charge a fee. On average all-day care is provided for two to three places per registered minder. The OPCS survey (Bone, 1977) suggests that about half of all minded children are under three.

Workplace nurseries - provided by employers for children of employees. They have a negligible effect on overall pre-school provision.

Private day nurseries - provided by child-care charities, colleges and local community groups but mostly privately. Children mostly attend full-time. General information on many aspects is not available.

On the basis of the latest statistics now available (1980)[1], these types of pre-school provide for 1,114,415 children, 41 per cent of which are provided for by local authorities and 59 per cent by voluntary or private agencies.

The proportion of under-fives attending the different types of provision

---

[1] Figures based on DHSS *Local Authority Social Service Statistics*, March 1980; DES *Statistical Bulletin*, January 1980, and Pre-school Playgroup Association 'Facts and Figures', 1980.

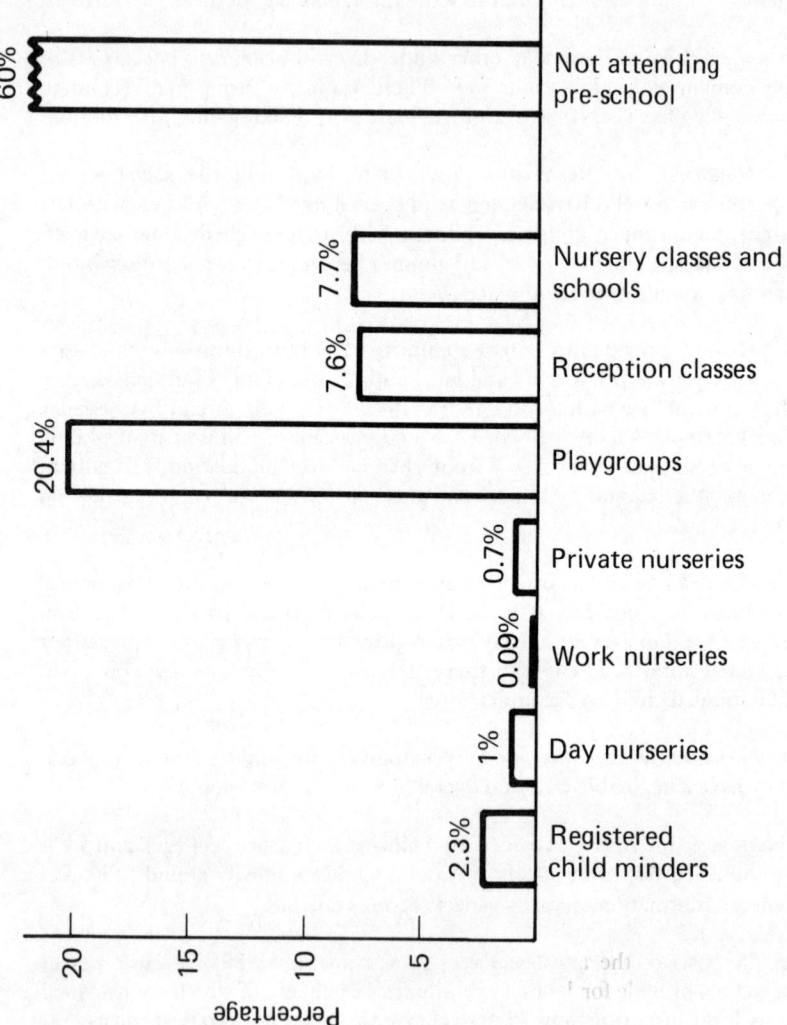

can also be calculated, and this is shown in Figure 1. Altogether some 40 per cent of under-fives attended some form of pre-school in 1977. Playgroups provided for most children, followed by classes in primary schools and then nursery classes/nursery schools. However, these percentages underestimate the extent of provision because they have been calculated on the basis of the *total* number of under-fives, yet most of the settings do not take children below the age of three. For nursery classes/nursery schools, playgroups, reception classes and day nurseries a fairer estimate would be the total number of attenders divided by the total number of three- and four-year-olds – an estimate that would bring the percentage of under-fives attending some form of pre-school provision to 74 per cent (*General Household Survey*, 1978).

The focus of the present study is on entry into pre-schools and so the ages at which children attend the different types of provision is of interest. Unfortunately statistics on this are not collected by some official sources, and so it is difficult to obtain a general and recent account. However, information collected in the *General Household Survey* was presented in these terms and it was found that attendance increased with the age of the child, as is shown in Figure 2. Ten per cent of one- to two-year-olds, and 74 per cent of three- to four-year-olds attended some form of pre-school.

The type of pre-school attended at each age level also varies, as is also shown in Figure 2. Playgroups and day nurseries took the bulk of nought- to two-year-olds whereas three- to four-year-olds were spread equally between these two (mainly playgroups) and schools.

2. Areas investigated in the study

The statistics on pre-school provision therefore show that the majority of children will at some point during their first four years enter a pre-school setting, though the type of setting and the age of entry vary enormously. Children can go straight from home into nursery classes/nursery schools, reception classes, playgroups or day nurseries, or they might go first to, say, a playgroup and then move on to a nursery class before entering a reception class. Other types of transition are also possible, and the overall pattern of transitions during the pre-school years is therefore complex and changing.

In this study we chose to concentrate on the transition of children from home into nursery class/nursery school. There were several reasons for this choice. In the first place, with inevitably limited research resources, it was thought preferable to gain an understanding of one form of transition in depth rather than obtain a superficial account of many. The transition from home to nursery classes/nursery schools is of special interest because it represents entry into the most well-established and 'educational' of the pre-school settings and one which is closely linked to the transition all children

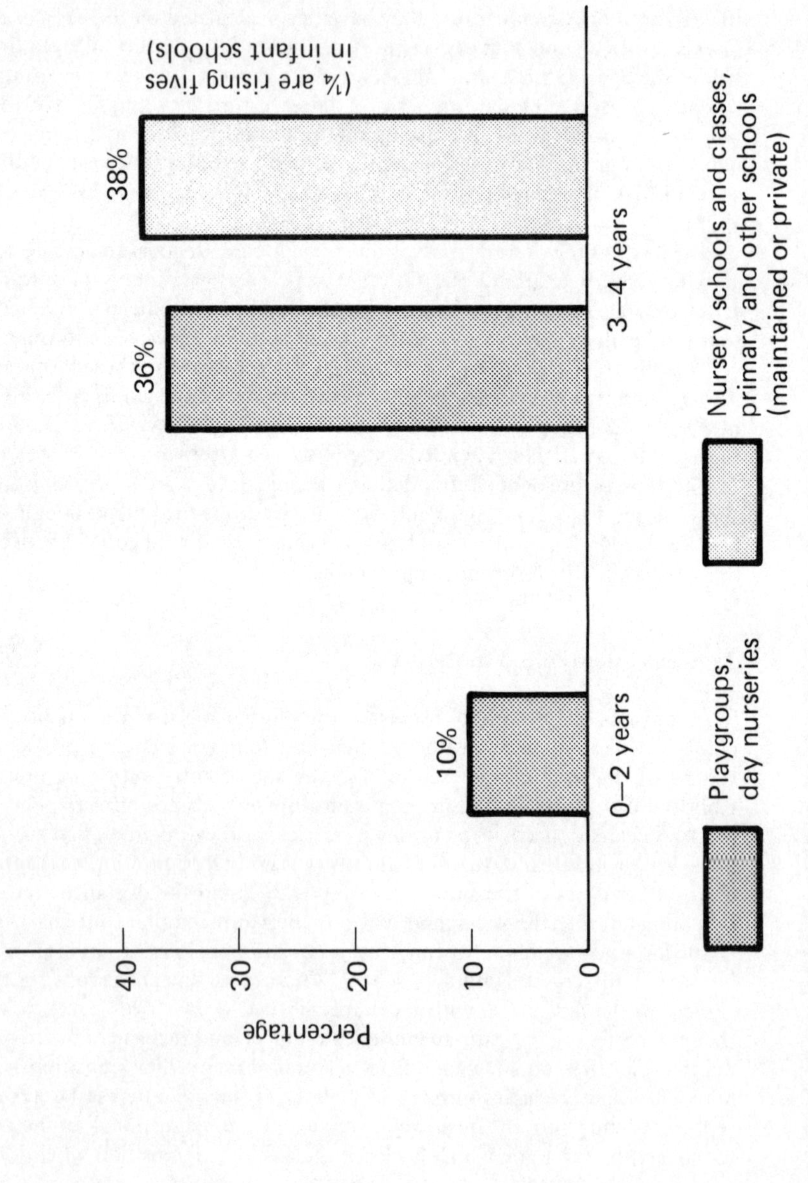

Percentage

40 —

30 —

20 —

10 —

0 —

0–2 years

3–4 years

10%

36%

38%
(½ are rising fives
in infant schools)

Playgroups,
day nurseries

Nursery schools and classes,
primary and other schools
(maintained or private)

will make when they begin attendance at primary schools. In addition, a series of studies concerned with nursery classes/nursery schools have been conducted at the NFER (Clift, Cleave and Griffin, 1980; Curtis and Blatchford, 1981; Curtis and Hill, 1978; Woodhead, 1976) and these studies provided a basis from which to investigate transition into this form of provision.

It was also anticipated that the issues involved would be similar to those occurring in transition to the other settings and would therefore elucidate general processes. Moreover, because of the prevalence of playgroups in the pre-school scene, they were also investigated from the point of view of transition, as we shall see below.

In keeping with our view that transition is best conceived as a continuous process, the study encompassed entry into pre-school, but also the situation prior to entry, as well as that in both nursery and home several months after entry. The investigation therefore looked at transition chronologically in terms of three areas:

i. prior to entry
ii. at the point of entry
iii. after entry

Our concern throughout was to elucidate and compare the perspectives of children, pre-school staff and parents at these three points.

We now look at these in depth, in the context of the research literature.

i. *Prior to entry*

CHILDREN
We can gain a fuller account of children's behaviour on entry if we have some appreciation of the kinds of experiences and environment they have encountered previously. Analyses of home backgrounds in the past have tended to be in terms of rather broad dimensions like social class, parental occupation, amenities in the home and overcrowding (e.g. Davie, Butler and Goldstein, 1972), or, conversely, in terms of specific aspects of child development such as language development (e.g. Wells, 1976; Wootton, 1974). White and his colleagues at Harvard have shown (1973, 1979) the value of a detailed observational investigation of the home as a learning environment.

It was not within our resources to provide a similarly exhaustive account but we did aim to describe children's lives in their homes, prior to entry into nursery, in a fashion that would highlight similarities and differences between the home and pre-school environments. Two broad areas were of interest. Firstly, one of the most immediate and concrete aspects of an environment is its *physical aspects*. It is this which sets the sensory boundaries to a child's experience. By 'physical aspects' we mean here aspects like the number and size of rooms the child will inhabit, as well as the presence and characteristics of outside areas. But physical aspects of a smaller scale are also likely to be influential, like the quantity and quality of play materials, including books, and the presence of television.

The second area of interest is the *social aspects* of the homes. It is through interactions with caretakers, siblings and others that the child will largely acquire language and, some would argue, these interactions will strongly influence his cognitive and social competence (Newson and Newson, 1975; White and Watts, 1973; Clarke-Stewart, 1973). In any case, social contacts are likely to differ from those at nursery and it is important to clarify in what ways. Accordingly, we set out to investigate the extent and type of contacts children experienced with their mothers, fathers and siblings, as well as those with adults and peers outside the home.

PRE-SCHOOL STAFF

There are a number of actions staff often take prior to children entering the nursery. The child's entry is likely to be influenced by these early steps. Preliminary visits to nursery schools and classes had already shown how carefully some staff had thought through first contacts with children and parents in order to ease transition and we wished to document these strategies.

Amongst topics of interest were the type of prior visits arranged to the nursery or even by staff to the children's homes and the type of information collected by staff from parents.

PARENTS

Another home influence on children will be their parents' attitudes and views toward their child's development. The extent to which these differ or match staffs' views and current practice is also relevant for it will figure in the adaptation of the child to the nursery. Amongst issues involved are the kinds of things parents feel it is important their children learn.

But parents' views toward pre-school attendance are of interest in their own right in order to clarify the extent to which the current situation adequately caters for their needs. As we have seen, nursery class and school attendance as well as playgroup attendance usually begins at three years at the earliest and is mostly part-time. We know that this situation is out of step with trends in female employment in the sense that mothers of pre-school children generally find it difficult to obtain suitable provision for them (see, e.g. Hughes *et al.*, 1980; Tizard, Moss and Perry, 1976). Within the context of the present topic, we were therefore interested in exploring in more detail parents' views on available provision.

One problem that has worried many people – especially those involved in health education – is the extent of parents' knowledge about facilities available for their pre-school children. Clearly there is a responsibility to ensure that the public understand the extent and type of provision available. We were therefore interested in establishing what parents know of pre-school provision and what provision if any they desired and for what reasons.

It will be seen below that information on the situation prior to entry was obtained from interviews and questionnaires from staff and parents. Results will be discussed in Chapters 2 and 3.

ii. *Entry*

CHILDREN

The way in which children respond to entry into nursery is obviously of prime concern. Despite its fundamental nature we were surprised to find only a handful of previous studies that had addressed it. If staff have acquired a knowledge of how children behave on entry, and how they might themselves act, it must have come largely from their own experiences and that of their colleagues because the contribution of research (though perhaps never as strong as researchers might like to believe) is in this case minimal. But with the growing sophistication of research and in particular observation techniques, research can make a strong contribution to our understanding of children's behaviour on entry. Questions which might usefully be addressed include, What changes in behaviour occur over the first weeks? How many children are upset as a result of separation from their parents? How many are aggressive or withdrawn?

Questions such as these were explored in an early unpublished study by Lena Baum conducted in the 1950s. Her main aim was to understand the means by which children learn to adapt to nursery school. She reported several stages in adjustment. At first children ignored the other children. Then they began watching what the others were doing, although withdrawing if approached and rarely interacting. When children did begin to interact, their contacts were at first clumsy and only became more purposeful and cooperative when they had some understanding of their own powers and rights in a situation. Success in adjusting to the group depended on the newcomer overcoming indifference or resentment from others.

With experience contacts became longer. At first they were of a simple approach-response type but later had a more complex pattern. First contacts with other children were found to occur more often in the presence of adults and to be initiated by the newcomers, not the established children. Comparison of a school which allowed mothers to stop with a school that did not suggested a number of differences in children's behaviour, including the finding that the former encouraged children to make more contacts, no doubt because children felt more secure – an interpretation one might make on the basis of psychological studies showing how children use their mothers as a secure base from which they can explore a strange environment (Ainsworth and Wittig, 1969; Rheingold, 1969). Baum suggests that interest in objects and toys precedes and encourages an interest in other children – a finding also found in the case of first contacts of younger children (e.g. Blatchford, 1979; Mueller and Lucas, 1975). Contacts therefore at first come about through toys but are later directly social. Baum also found that children in the nursery where the mothers stayed showed less signs of distress on arrival.

Much of Baum's study rested on informal comment rather than systematically collected data and the same must be said of another interesting study by Janis (1964). This book is a case study of the separation reactions of a two-year-old on entry into nursery school. The author was a friend of the child's family and able to observe the child throughout the nursery year at home, as well as hold frequent discussions with the mother and interview the nursery teacher. The child's behaviour was interpreted largely in terms of Freudian theory and followed the works of Bowlby and Robertson on the effects on children of separation from their mothers. The child's sometimes painful separation from her mother and gradual adjustment to the nursery school and the teacher is meticulously and sensitively described.

Mention must also be made of a study by Dorothy May (1963). Though not principally concerned with entry as such – it is an account of problems faced by children in their personal and social adjustment to nursery school – it contains a wealth of informed description and interpretation from an experienced teacher that is relevant to entry.

In contrast to the interpretive works of Janis and May, a more recent study by McGrew (1972) has been careful, consistent with the tradition of ethology, to restrict itself to an objective description of children's behaviour. McGrew observed 12 children during their first five days at nursery and then again three months later. He found the behaviour of newcomers varied widely though there was an increase after entry in social and aggressive behaviour. McGrew found that newcomers were behaviourally indistinguishable from the others after approximately 65 days of nursery experience.

Feldbaum, Christensen and O'Neal (1980) also observed 12 newcomers, this time into three pre-schools, for four weeks after entry. Newcomers exhibited more isolation and 'off-task' behaviour while established children engaged in more parallel and cooperative play, and verbalizing with peers. Sex differences were found: girl newcomers were more orientated toward teachers, boy newcomers were more interested in other boys. Perhaps as a result, girls took longer to become assimilated into the group.

It can be seen that studies of children entering pre-school have been either of a qualitative kind or, in the case of the studies of McGrew and Feldbaum *et al.*, based exclusively on systematic observational data on a small sample. Neither of the two latter studies had much to say about individual differences in the reaction of children to entry. Information on this, however, is likely to have a practical bearing on the strategies adopted by staff.

Our aim was to help answer the basic question of how children behave on entry into pre-school by studying a larger sample of children on the basis of a broader range of variables. Systematic observations on children were conducted because of their capacity of providing detailed and reliable quantitative data on children, but other research instruments were also used, i.e. a test of children's conceptual ability and measures of children's adjustment to nursery, as seen by staff.

We set out to build up a picture of just how children behave on entry into nursery by addressing the following questions:

- How is children's behaviour distributed on entry between adults, other children and equipment?
- Do children have distinctive styles of behaviour toward adults, other children and equipment?
- Does their behaviour change over time in the nursery and if so how?
- To what extent is children's behaviour on entry associated with their home background and previous experiences?

With regard to the last question, previous work suggests wide individual differences in children's reactions to entry (May, 1963). In the above section on 'Prior to entry', we have spoken of a general description of the social, physical and attitudinal aspects of homes, but these too are likely to differ. One important question therefore concerns the extent to which different children's reactions are associated with different previous experiences.

There is a good deal of evidence now available showing that early experiences are indeed associated with many aspects of the child's development. Some studies, for example, have found associations between social class, parental education, household amenities and overcrowding on the one hand and measures of a child's attainment and adjustment at primary school on the other (e.g. Davie, Butler and Goldstein, 1972; Plowden Report, 1967). Other studies have shown associations between measures of home life (especially maternal social interaction with the child), and measures of a child's intellectual, social and linguistic functioning, to be evident as early as the first two years of life (e.g. Clarke-Stewart, 1973). There is also an established literature showing that children from backgrounds designated as socially or culturally deprived tend to show inferior performances when compared with children from non-disadvantaged homes on a number of linguistic, intellectual and social measures (e.g. Phillips *et al.*, 1972; Smilansky, 1968; Tough, 1977).

Finally, Caldwell and her colleagues devised a means of measuring the home as a learning environment (the 'HOME' schedule) and have found significant correlations between this measure and pre-school children's linguistic development (Elardo, Bradley and Caldwell, 1977) and IQ (Bradley and Caldwell, 1976).

On the basis of these results it seems reasonable to inquire whether children's home background and experiences are associated with their behaviour outside the home in pre-school settings. It is odd, when one considers the vast number of studies of children's behaviour at pre-school, dating back to the early direct observational studies of children's behaviour conducted during the 1930s and 1940s (see reviews by Arrington, 1943; Wright, 1966), and which have now been supplemented by studies from an ethological perspective (e.g. Blurton Jones, 1972), that few relationships between behaviour and earlier experience have been investigated. Several studies, though, do provide clues. Lieberman (1977) found that competence of three-year-olds in contacting peers was associated, though in different ways, with security of attachment to mother and the amount of prior contact with peers; the former was associated with non-verbal, and the latter with verbal measures of peer competence. Further analysis also showed that maternal attitudes toward the child's expression of aggression and freedom to explore were significantly correlated with the child's social competence with other children.

Looking at this type of association more specifically, Endsley *et al.* (1979) found relationships between certain maternal interaction patterns and children's curiosity in a semi-structured laboratory situation. In particular, the frequency with which mothers interested their children in the exploration of novel materials, responded positively to their exploration, answered their questions, and explored the novel objects themselves, was significantly associated with their children's curiosity, measured in terms of exploration and questions.

Previous research, though far from conclusive, therefore suggests a number of ways in which children's previous experiences might be associated with their behaviour at nursery. In particular, children's contacts with their parents and the extent of their previous social experience outside the home appear to be influential. It was our aim to explore these associations more fully by collecting information on children's home background in order to search for associations with their behaviour at nursery.

Results of the issues raised on children's entry into pre-school, discussed in this section, will be presented in Chapters 4 and 5.

STAFF STRATEGIES

If research, as we have said, has not been very informative about children's reactions to entry there is little doubt that nursery staff have taken notice of such reactions and devised strategies to help children settle. We were interested in documenting staffs' views, not only on children's behaviour and how they dealt with it, but also on organizational factors such as visits to the nursery. These are discussed in Chapter 2.

PARENTS

Finally, children are not the only ones who may be disorientated by entry. Indeed, early discussions with staff indicate that problems of adjustment were sometimes attributable to parents', and especially mothers', distress. In the interest of examining children's behaviour it is all too easy to overlook the very real problems that may face mothers in the face of what may be a threatening time. Understanding their reactions may help foster a more positive climate for all concerned. These are discussed in Chapter 6.

iii. *After entry*

CHILDREN
As we have said, transition is a continuous process that extends beyond the point of entry. It is important to take a longer term perspective on children's behaviour. Having described patterns of behaviour on entry we must study their ensuing development in order to establish how long it takes children to adapt to the nursery and in what ways this takes place. This longer term perspective should also help establish the extent to which early problems of adjustment, as seen for instance in distressed or aggressive behaviour, are reflected in later behaviour. Are these behaviours, for instance, a reliable predictor of later problems? On the other hand it may be that some behaviours tend to 'wash out' after a time at nursery. Identification of behaviour patterns that are of an enduring nature should help separate out relatively deep-rooted from short-term behaviours and hence be informative about which behaviours signal the need for special attention. Another possibility, of course, is that problems of adjustment may only manifest themselves after the lapse of several weeks or so.

STAFF
In one sense transition from home to pre-school is unique in that children do not so much leave one setting for another – for example pre-school to primary school or primary to secondary – but continue to be strongly influenced, at such a dependant age, by their home experiences. This places great stress on the kind of relationship that exists between the home and pre-school settings.
  Issues of interest include:

- What kinds of relations exist between staff and parents after entry?
- What type of formal contact takes place, e.g. open days or talks, and what is the nature and extent of informal contacts?
- To what extent do parents help in the nursery and what is the reality of parental involvement in day to day life in the pre-school?

Parental involvement in primary schools has been the subject of recent research (Cyster, Clift and Battle, 1980; Tizard *et al.*, 1981). It was not within our power to study the topic in similar depth, though we did assess its bearing on transition. This is discussed in Chapter 2.

PARENTS
Clearly it would be of only limited value to attend to the child's adjustment

to nursery if we have no idea of what is thought by those in the home. As we have said, children after entry will still spend the bulk of their time in the home environment and the attitudes and opinions of those there will affect the child's own attitudes. So we set out to establish parents' views on the child's life at nursery: in what ways, if any, the experience had affected the child's life at home and how had it affected parents, in practical and personal terms. Discussions of parents' views after entry can be found in Chapter 6.

Summary of areas to be investigated

The study was designed to investigate the following areas:

a. PRIOR TO ENTRY
Children: a description of physical and social aspects of their home environment.
Staff: actions taken by staff prior to children entering the nursery. First contacts between staff, parents and children, e.g. prior visits to the nursery and information collected on children.
Parents: views about, and knowledge of, pre-school provision.

b. ENTRY
Children: how do they behave on entry into the nursery? Are there noticeable individual differences in behaviour? Does behaviour change over time after entry? To what extent is behaviour associated with home background and previous experiences?
Staff: strategies adopted by staff to help children settle into pre-school.
Parents: reactions of parents to their child's entry into pre-school.

c. AFTER ENTRY
Children: how does behaviour change with time in the nursery?
Staff: what are staffs' attitudes and actions toward parental involvement in the nursery?
Parents: how do parents view their child's life at nursery? How has it affected them and their child's behaviour at home?

3. **Research design**

In order to study the three areas – prior to entry, entry, after entry – a variety of methods were used and are now briefly described. Fuller details are presented where the relevant results are discussed in later chapters. The overall research design is shown in Figure 3.

i. *Information on children*

OBSERVATIONAL STUDY

The behaviour of newcomers into nursery classes in two local education authorities was studied in depth by a direct observational study. An observation schedule was used to code each child's behaviour toward adults, other children and equipment in free play, and another schedule coded children's behaviour in sessions like story and music that were directed by staff. More open-ended notes were taken in order to build up case studies of a small number of children. Children were observed every day for the first three weeks at nursery and then again for the whole of their ninth week there.

TESTS AND ADJUSTMENT QUESTIONNAIRES

Information on the children's basic conceptual ability was obtained by administering the McCarthy Scale of Mental Ability and information on how each adjusted to nursery was obtained from a questionnaire completed by staff.

ii. *Information from parents*

PARENT INTERVIEWS

Prior to the children's entry their parents were interviewed. Information was collected on the home environment from the point of view of its social (e.g. frequency and type of social contacts), physical (e.g. toys, books, number of rooms) and 'attitudinal' characteristics. We also obtained information on children's daily life in the home and parents' knowledge of, and attitudes toward, pre-school provision.

In order to obtain a larger sample of parents for the purpose of a more comprehensive coverage, a separate group of parents, whose children were not subsequently observed, was also interviewed.

Parents who had been interviewed prior to their children entering nurseries were interviewed about their impressions of how they and their children had reacted to entry and any changes they had noticed in their children's behaviour at home. Information was obtained on their relationship with the nursery and their satisfaction with information on, and discussion of, the progress of their children.

iii. *Information from staff*

NURSERY SCHOOL AND CLASS INTERVIEWS AND QUESTIONNAIRES

Interviews and questionnaires were used to obtain information on a number of issues from staff in different areas in England. These included a description of the social, physical and attitudinal characteristics of the nursery, strategies adopted prior to entry (e.g. pre-visits), type of information required on children from parents, strategies to help children settle and contacts with parents after their child's entry.

PLAYGROUP QUESTIONNAIRE
Questionnaires were sent to a sample of playgroups addressing similar issues to those asked of nursery staff.

Full details of the research instruments used and the results from them are discussed in the following chapters.

4. Structure of the report

The description of the research design seen in Figure 3 also shows how we decided to structure our report: we have chronologically followed the steps involved in a child's transition from home to pre-school, and we have followed the sequence of areas to be investigated, presented above. Chapter 3 discusses the situation prior to entry. Essentially this stems from our interviews with parents.

Chapter 4 is a central chapter in the book because it describes children's entry into nursery. We present here data from the observational study, the tests and adjustment questionnaires.

In Chapter 5 we provide a complementary account on children's entry by presenting case studies of four children, representative of the different styles of reaction we found. These case studies are based on the observational data and also information from the children's parents and staff.

Chapter 6 is concerned with the parents' perspective after entry.

In Chapter 7, we summarize some of our findings putting forward conclusions about transition from home to pre-school in the context of a general review of available provision, and emphasizing the importance of inter-relationships between children, staff and parents in any assessment of transition.

To set these chapters into perspective we first provide in Chapter 2 a general account of transition – a broad sweep as it were – that came from the interviews with, and questionnaires to, staff in nursery classes and schools, and playgroups.

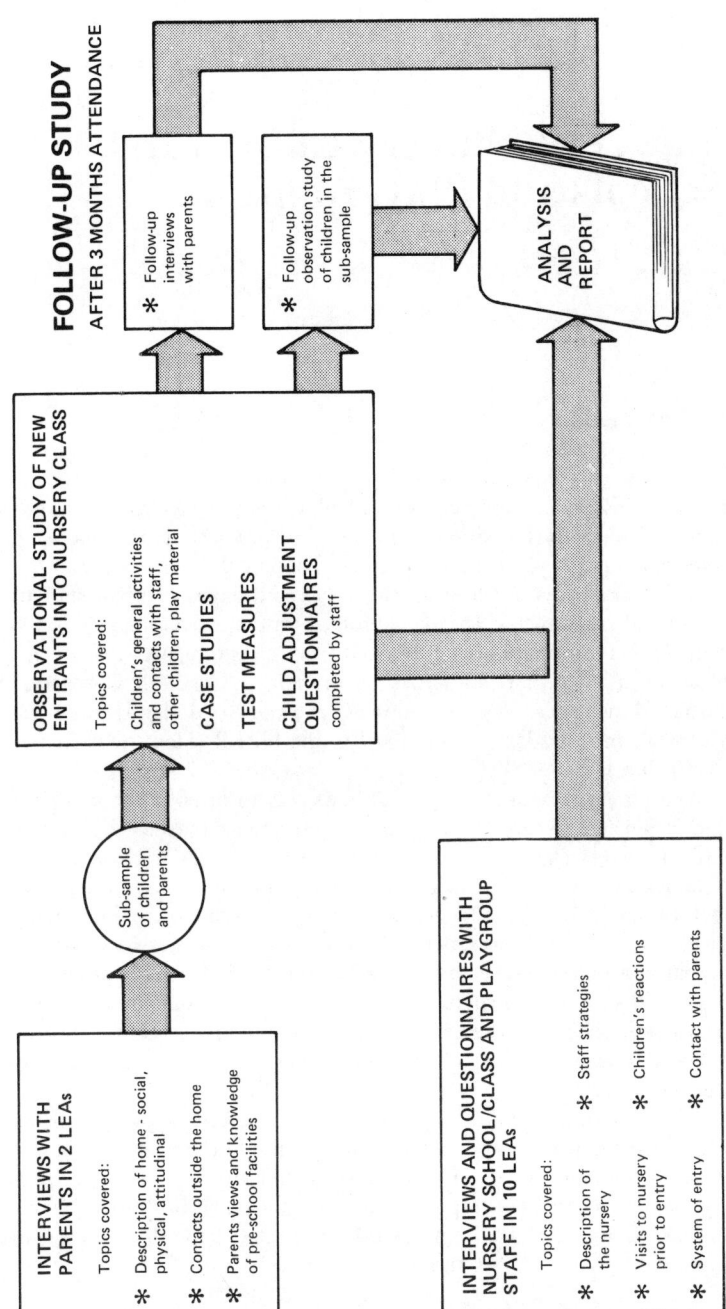

PRIOR TO ENTRY

INTERVIEWS WITH
PARENTS IN 2 LEAs

Topics covered:

* Description of home - social,
physical, attitudinal

* Contacts outside the home

* Parents views and knowledge
of pre-school facilities

INTERVIEWS AND QUESTIONNAIRES WITH
NURSERY SCHOOL/CLASS AND PLAYGROUP
STAFF IN 10 LEAs

Topics covered:

* Description of   * Staff strategies
the nursery

* Visits to nursery   * Children's reactions
prior to entry

* System of entry   * Contact with parents

Sub-sample
of children
and parents

ENTRY INTO NURSERY CLASS

OBSERVATIONAL STUDY OF NEW
ENTRANTS INTO NURSERY CLASS

Topics covered:

Children's general activities
and contacts with staff,
other children, play material

CASE STUDIES

TEST MEASURES

CHILD ADJUSTMENT
QUESTIONNAIRES
completed by staff

FOLLOW-UP STUDY

AFTER 3 MONTHS ATTENDANCE

* Follow-up
interviews
with parents

* Follow-up
observation study
of children in the
sub-sample

ANALYSIS
AND
REPORT

CHAPTER 2

Survey of Nursery Classes and Schools and Playgroups

1. Introduction

The aim of this chapter is to describe information we collected from staff in nursery classes, nursery schools and playgroups concerning a number of issues involved in transition from home to pre-school. In contrast to the intensive studies reported in ensuing chapters the aim here was to get a general perspective by hearing the views and experiences of staff from a number of areas on a wide range of topics. In the case of nursery classes and schools this information was obtained from questionnaires to staff in seven local education authorities (LEAs) (Birmingham, Cornwall, Coventry, Doncaster, Manchester, Newcastle-upon-Tyne and Sunderland) and interviews with staff in three LEAs more local to the NFER (Hounslow, Surrey and Hampshire).

The reason for conducting interviews was to provide the more detailed and responsive picture that can only stem from face to face discussion. In the case of nursery classes we usually interviewed the head of the main school - whether it be infant or all-through primary - and then moved on to interview staff in the nursery class. In the case of nursery schools, we interviewed the head teacher. The interviews were then processed in two ways: firstly a verbatim account and secondly a 'grid' to provide basic quantitative information that exactly matched that from the questionnaires. Quantitative information from both sources was then combined. Altogether, information from 171 nurseries was collected (a response rate of 88 per cent for the questionnaires).

In addition, questionnaires were sent to a sample of playgroups in four areas that were the same as the nursery sample (Doncaster, Manchester, Newcastle-upon-Tyne and Sunderland). Seventy-two of these questionnaires were returned (a response rate of 68 per cent). In this chapter we will discuss the main themes. Unless otherwise stated the discussion concerns nurseries (nursery classes and nursery schools).

2. Contacts prior to entry

Putting the child's name on the waiting list

Perhaps the first question which might be asked concerns how parents come to hear about the nursery. None of our interview respondents advertised their nursery in any way; in all cases parents came to hear about the nursery through word of mouth. One does wonder to what extent this evenly communicates the presence of the nursery to its surrounding community. On the other hand many nurseries had long waiting lists, and few appeared to have numbers below their official placement size, and so it is little surprise that no one identified this as a problem.

There did not appear to be a clear pattern in the age at which a child's name was allowed to be put down on the waiting list. About one-third of the total sample of nurseries did prefer a child's name to be put down after his second birthday. This was reported to be because of the already heavy demand on places and the need to keep the waiting list to manageable proportions, but also because some staff had learnt through experience that quite a lot may happen over the space of a couple of years – families may move, for example, or parents may find alternative pre-school provision for their child – and thus a waiting list may not be very accurate by the time children are of an age to attend the nursery.

The majority of schools on the other hand (perhaps those with a less pressing demand on places) adopted a more *laissez-faire* attitude and left the time of putting a child's name down to parents. One head considered that she must have broken some kind of record in this regard. One morning she received an excited message from a girl in the infant school, 'Mummy's just had a little boy and she wants you to put his name down on the nursery waiting list!'

Types of entrant

The first contact, then, between parent and schools occurs when the child's name is put down on the waiting list. There are three types of entrant. In the first place there are the usually sizeable proportion whose parents already have, or have had, other children in the school, and where the child's name is put down as a matter of course, perhaps when the older children are collected. Several heads indicated that this was usually an informal and brief occasion. It is also likely in such cases that the prospective nursery child will already have visited the school and be acquainted with classrooms and staff. A second category is very different. These are cases referred by agencies such as health visitors, social workers, local GPs and speech therapists, as in special need of nursery provision. On hearing from staff of the wide variety of reasons behind this need, we received a vivid and often disturbing picture of modern urban life. All schools have a responsibility to take a proportion of such emergency cases. The third category were those whose parents were previously unacquainted with the nursery and now desired to put their child's name down. These might hear of the nursery from other mothers, health visitors and, in a few cases, they might contact the education office.

Visits prior to entry

Having put the child's name down, what then happens before the actual day of entry? Our question to this effect revealed a varied picture. One dimension of variance is the extent of contact: 89 per cent of nurseries invited all parents and children to visit the school, whilst the rare school organized no further contact at all until the day of entry. Some schools laid on an extensive series of pre-visits in order to acquaint child and mother with the nursery. The degree of formality attached by the school to pre-visits is another dimension of variance, as shown in Table 2.1. Some adopt an informal attitude, perhaps giving mothers an open invitation to drop into the nursery whenever they like, whilst others try their best to ensure all mothers come to perhaps a pre-arranged talk by the head and a more formally guided visit to the nursery.

Table 2.1: Type of prior visit to nursery (n = 130)

	%[1]
Meeting of a group of mothers with staff	2
Discussion and short group visit to nursery	4
Discussion and longer group visit to nursery	6
Individual discussion with head or teacher	2
Individual discussion with head or teacher and short visit to nursery	31
Individual discussion with head and longer visit to nursery (e.g. an hour or several visits)	31
Visit nursery for an afternoon or morning	15
Other scheme	11

[1] In this and other tables, percentages have been rounded up or down and may not therefore exactly total 100%.

It is our impression that although the informal approach may be guided by a commendable desire for mothers to initiate their own degree of involvement, without a certain amount of encouragement, some parents will feel disinclined to visit the school at their own volition. Moreover, it is likely to be parents who, from staff's point of view, would most benefit from acquaintance with the nursery who are least likely to come.

The two most typical types of pre-visits are for an individual mother and child pair to visit the nursery for either a short or longer visit sometime in the term prior to the official day of entry, as well as having an individual discussion with the head or teacher. Often the school ensures that the visitors experience the session (i.e. morning or afternoon) that the child is due to attend – a sound idea in view of the usually completely different group of children in each session and the reports we have commonly heard about the different character of the sessions. Sometimes either the head or the teacher in charge of the nursery will give a talk in order to prepare parents for the day of entry. This might simply cover basic information on the school and its rules or it might be a longer session within which the school's philosophy is explained in depth and parents are encouraged to ask questions. During one visit to a school in Southampton the interviewer sat in one one of these latter sessions. A nursery was organized so that a nursery teacher could talk to a group of mothers of children due to attend the nursery the next term. The talk was informal but instructive. First the teacher described to parents what they should expect on the days after entry and what they might do, and then parents were encouraged to ask questions. Because of the amount of time given to parents, and the explicit way the child's nursery life was discussed, parents had a clear understanding of what they might expect and what they might contribute, as well as the beginning of a communicative relationship with staff. It is important that someone takes a lead in this way. In our experience staff as well as parents can lack the confidence to address directly issues concerning the child's life at nursery.

During these pre-visits children may spend the bulk of their time by their mother's side. Sometimes, however, they may be encouraged to explore the nursery environment. Having a spare room to which mothers can go for coffee can be useful here because a child can then explore the nursery on his own but feel secure in the knowledge that his mother is still on hand if he should need her.

But prior contacts with parents and children need not take place on school premises. Some staff are now meeting parents and child in the parental home. In 33 per cent of nurseries and 26 per cent of playgroups such visits were conducted. Of the staff undertaking such a system, the majority found them valuable. Most felt that they helped to get to know the child individually in a way that would not be possible on the basis of the inevitably busy first day of entry. The visits can also be valuable because they can help to create a trusting and more natural relationship with parents. Parents may feel rather inhibited at school and should be more inclined to relax in their home territory. Every teacher in the interview sample who tried home visits reported a favourable response from parents. Contrary to fears that we have heard expressed, virtually every parent welcomed the teacher and offered her the ubiquitous cup of tea. One teacher found a good response in a nursery situation comprising 98 per cent Asian children. She said:

I visit the home before the child comes to school. The reason for this is in order that the child will accept me as a friend. It also creates good relations with parents. I sometimes take something for the child to do in the home, because they don't seem to get much to do at all. I'm accepted 99 per cent of the time. But I have to accept them as they are. I'm always offered tea – I don't like this because they always add sugar and I don't like sugar, but I always drink it because I don't want to offend them. At the meeting I offer them a place and give them a letter. I ask them to come to the nursery with their birth certificate and then also ask for quite a lot of details.

Another teacher did remark that she felt far more comfortable on these visits if she felt she had a reason for being there. Because of this she took it upon herself to tell parents about the school, give them a pamphlet on the school, and complete a form with them, listing basic information on the child.

In one Hounslow infant school the two nursery teachers divided a list of September's intake in two, and made a point of visiting each child and mother on their list during the previous summer term. They devoted much effort to ensuring that these visits were a success. One made a point of taking an interest in the child. Her ploy was to sit on a settee and invite the child to sit next to her. She could then ask the child what he would like to do in the nursery and what toys he would like to play with, and these could then be put out when he arrived for a prior visit. This immediately gave the child a focus of interest in the strange environment and ensured that he would feel some control over it.

Some may not consider home visits practical or even desirable but it is certainly a promising method that might be tried more widely. It has the special merit of taking the school to the home and thereby making it more accessible to parents and child at the very beginning of the child's school life. This may go some way toward involving parents in the child's education at the very beginning. But the converse point might also be made: it shows a willingness on the school's part to involve itself in the community.

In one school a system was adopted which blurred the distinction between pre-visits and a 'staggered entry' system (entering children in small groups – this will be discussed shortly). For the first half of a term, parents brought their children for two sessions per week. Mothers were in all cases required to stay in the nursery and in the case of a child in care a member of staff was asked to accompany her. This particular nursery was a separate nursery school housed in a large Victorian house and was lucky enough to have an extra room upstairs. After five or six weeks the newcomers' mothers were encouraged to go to this room in order to enable their child to more freely explore the nursery. This was deliberately called the 'half way' stage and, if all went well, the number of days' attendance was quickly increased to three, four and finally five days. By this time children were usually eagerly inquiring if they could come every day. Quite deliberately the policy was to increase child attendance and concurrently decrease parental attendance. Not surprisingly the teacher in charge of this school reported no signs of upset on entry. She said, 'That's the whole point of the exercise'. Also parents have been very closely involved in their child's new experience and in helping him settle.

It can therefore be seen that a wide variety of prior contacts exist. The lack of standardization is quite in keeping with the need for flexibility and experimentation. It would be wrong to attempt to identify better or worse methods, but it *is* important that staff are aware of different possibilities and have considered what system might be best for their particular circumstances. In some cases we did feel that a system existed more by tradition or for the sake of administrative convenience than in the interests of child or parent.

3. Information prior to entry

Virtually all schools and playgroups felt obliged to collect certain basic information on children, as seen in Table 2.2. In the case of nurseries, this would typically be collected from mothers during one of her visits prior to entry and might include the child's date of birth, the address and telephone number, the parents' place of employment in case of emergency, and the name of the family GP. This was usually, but not always, collected on a printed form.

Table 2.2: Information required from parents prior to entry.

	Nurseries (n = 170)	Playgroups (n = 72)
	%	%
Basic biographical details and also further details, e.g. medical	69	93
Basic biographical details only	28	4
None collected	3	3

Although some nursery respondents thought that there was some kind of directive from their LEA about what information to collect, many appeared unsure and information that was collected therefore resulted from their own initiative.

Any further information that was collected was usually of a more informal kind, and might result from such a prompt as, 'and is there anything else you think we ought to know . . .?' Schools varied in their attitudes to further information gathering. A few schools, for example, felt consciously disinclined to collect much information from parents on the grounds that they did not have the right or that it was unnecessary. At the other extreme were those schools who consciously tried to get as much information as possible, usually because they felt it was in the child's best interests for as much as possible to be known about him. But perhaps the bulk of schools did not appear to have a conscious policy and recorded further information as and when it came up. (As an aside it might be noted that written information on schools and playgroups was given to *parents* by 61 per cent of nurseries and 60 per cent of playgroups.)

Types of further information collected included any health problems, e.g. whether the child had had any serious illness or had any allergies, and details of family circumstances, e.g. whether it was a single parent family. Apart from schools in one LEA who were complying with their chief education officer on a study of the subject, few schools made a point of collecting information on children's previous pre-school experiences. In some cases it was known if the child had attended a playgroup but knowledge was very hazy on whether children had been minded or had been to other pre-school settings like mother and toddler clubs. Considering that several respondents mentioned differences between playgroup and non-playgroup experienced children, this kind of information perhaps ought to be given a higher priority.

One might think that the most detailed information would be available on children who had been referred to the nursery, e.g. by health visitors or social services, but this was not necessarily the case; for example, a 'referral' would involve a hurried phone call to the head asking whether she had room for a certain child. We got the impression that this was not often followed by a written report giving further details, though one head did tell us she had received a very detailed and comprehensive report on one child from a community physician.

A number of people are now stressing the need for greater cooperation between the various agencies concerned with the pre-school child, e.g. schools, social services, doctors and playgroups. In view of this we asked questions about contacts schools had with other agencies. The amount of information received from them is shown in Table 2.3. It can be seen that nurseries have rather more contact than playgroups with health visitors and social workers. It was our impression that contacts were still very thin on the ground and usually only occurred in the case of an emergency. A few heads complained about being inadequately informed about some children. Doctors were especially singled out for still sticking rigidly to the concept of confidentiality of information. We were given several examples of situations where a school really needed to have more medical information in order to deal appropriately with a child. One child, for example, was only later found to have asthma and another child a form of epilepsy. For the child's sake, schools really need to be adequately prepared to deal with cases like these. Of course the problem as far as schools are concerned does not only involve medical agencies. We heard several times that parents had withheld information about their child, presumably for fear that the child might not get a place in the nursery or that he might be considered somehow odd. On the other hand there is also the possibility that parents may not consider certain experiences relevant to a head's inquiries. One head gave a hypothetical example of this. To the head's inquiry 'has your child spent any time away from you, has she been hospitalized at all?', a mother might reply, 'oh no, only when she was fostered for two years!'

Table 2.3: Information received from other agencies.

	NURSERY					PLAYGROUP				
	Often	Some-times	Rarely	Never	n	Often	Some-times	Rarely	Never	n
	%	%	%	%		%	%	%	%	
Health visitor	19	51	20	11	161	10	29	30	31	70
Social worker	7	45	29	18	163	6	34	29	31	70
Other parents	4	18	20	59	164	11	21	13	54	70
Previous playgroup	6	10	17	67	163	–	4	4	91	70
Others	7	15	13	65	164	6	10	1	82	68

In general, therefore, recognition of the need for greater cooperation between pre-school agencies was still a long way from actuality, at least at the level of consultation involving schools. But having said this, there were quite clear indications that changes were taking place. Several heads in one major city considered that they now had very healthy contacts with health visitors and social service departments. One head was especially pleased at the willingness to include her in case conferences. As she said, 'After all, it's crazy that we aren't invited when we have to look after the child's day to day needs. There was one case involving non-accidental injury when I was the person who advised social services about the child! In this case it would have been absurd if I had not been included in the case conference.' Another head also detected a greater willingness to set up channels of communication between different agencies. She had recently been to a conference organized locally and found it very illuminating. The main value of this meeting had been to hear from other agencies about their responsibilities and feelings about current issues. Although only a first step, all had apparently come away with a clearer picture of the field and who might best be qualified to deal with particular problems. One head remarked that the change was most evident in the social services. She remarked that at a recent meeting she had asked whether they might receive more detailed information in writing about 'emergency' children from the social services. The answer to this question was still in the negative but it was noticeable that the attitude had softened over the past two years. As she said, 'it may be the Maria Caldwell case that has affected opinion at the top – I'm not sure – but when they get to know you, and realize that you're not prying, they'll give you more information – they recognize that it's in the child's best interest'.

Changes were also evident in the actual mechanics of collecting information. Some areas, for example, had set up formal inquiries into the best method of standardizing information gathered about children. Some areas were also about to implement new record cards that demanded more background information on children.

Overall, though, we felt that the type and extent of prior information collected was an area in need of careful consideration. We felt that the information collected in some schools was, from an outsider's point of view, rather sketchy and there was often a rather uncritical assessment on schools' part about what information might be worth obtaining and ways in which this might be achieved.

It is important to recognize that the prior information issue is not simply a matter of academic concern but one of some practical significance. We have heard it said that there is little need for information on a child because one learns soon enough about him, and in any case it can set up presuppositions about a child's behaviour that might prejudice staff's behaviour. But this view is rather narrow-minded. It presupposes that children can be left at the door of a school and then be expected to live in two separate worlds with little knowledge of each other. Segmentation of this kind can do little to aid a child's progress at school and staff really need to consider a dialogue with others, including parents, in order that they might best steer the nursery environment to meet children's individual needs.

4. Procedures on entry

So what strategies did staff adopt when children entered pre-school?

Staggered entry

The most basic method employed in order to help children settle into nursery was a staggered entry, where the termly intake was divided up into small groups of children and these then entered at intervals. The rationale for this procedure is that staff will be able to help a few newcomers settle before the rest come in. (The fact that less than half the playgroups – 49 per cent – operated a staggered entry system is no doubt associated with the fact that entry was most likely to be continuous throughout the year and not termly – 31 per cent of playgroups – or yearly – only 10 per cent of playgroups.) The basic assumption is that having all the newcomers on the first day would encourage children to be upset (one child's upset could affect others) and staff would find it difficult to cope. The word 'assumption' is used here because virtually no one had ever directly experienced such a situation. It must also be noted that in most nurseries a large majority of the children coming in each term were not newcomers but children who had already spent at least a term in the nursery. Rarely would a nursery group therefore start from scratch, as it were.

Although the staggered system was widely adopted, details of implementation varied. The number of children who entered each session varied from as few as two to as many as 20, with an average being around six. In the case of one school where six children entered in one session there was a clear difference of opinion between the head and the teacher in charge of the nursery. It was the teacher's view that six was far too many at once and that she did not have time to settle these before the next group entered. For the head, on the other hand, the present system was much easier to organize.

Another difference concerned the days of entry. Most nurseries preferred to enter the newcomers after the 'old stagers' had had a chance to re-settle for a few days. In the case of a nursery class, the nursery newcomers would therefore also enter after the main school had been back for a few days. Nurseries also differed in terms of whether entries were on consecutive days (34 per cent) or whether there were gaps of two days or more between entries (66 per cent), and this in turn affected how long it took to enter all the newcomers – a range from a few days to an entire term, with an average of 15 days. A few schools seemed to feel that entering children on Mondays was rather chancing fate and made every effort to avoid it. But some schools were more concerned not to enter children on Friday because the weekend break would interrupt the continuity of the settling in process. Obviously the operational details adopted were conditioned by the school's 'policy', but were also more simply affected by the numbers of children entering each term. In connection with this point the number of entries varied within as well as between schools, with the summer term usually having fewer entries.

Before we leave this account of staggered entry, it is worth recounting the novel procedure being used by one nursery teacher in an infant/junior school who was allowed a good deal of autonomy by her head. (As an aside, we often found nursery staff in all-through primary schools were given more autonomy than those in infant schools – most probably because in a larger unit the head would be more inclined to delegate responsibility to his staff. But we also found that heads of junior/infant schools were more likely to be male than those of infant schools and, in our experience, appeared to feel less at home in the nursery.) This teacher had inverted the normal entry procedure: in contrast to normal practice all the newcomers entered in the first day and the old stagers entered at a later point. At first glance we thought this would be a recipe for disaster but the teacher had good reasons for her system and she felt that it worked well. Her view was that it allowed the newcomer to look around without interference from a lot of other boisterous 'old stagers', and that it gave staff a chance to observe them closely and give them more attention. In the teacher's words they 'are not lost in a crowd'. This was also a splendid system from a mother's point of view because she did not apparently feel so awful if her child cried, she found it easier to approach staff, and she felt easier about staying in the nursery than she would if a host of other mothers left. The teacher also felt that she was more likely to hear from mothers about the child's 'little quirks' – clearly knowledge that would better enable staff to deal with the child appropriately. No doubt many would expect this system to have its drawbacks – e.g. what of the newcomers' new-found peace on the morning when they are invaded by a host of usually older children? – but the fact that it seemed to work in this case suggests the value of experimentation in this area.

Mothers staying after entry

Apart from staggered entry there is one other main way that pre-schools usually attempt to help children settle. This involves asking mothers to stay for a while on their child's first days. Once again the rationale is simple. It is felt that children will more easily settle into a strange environment if they have a familiar figure there also. But there was a far more marked difference of opinion about the value of this than was the case with staggered entry. With regard to nurseries, opinions fell into three categories (see Table 2.4). In the first place there were those who asked mothers to stay as a deliberate policy and would insist they did so even if a mother wanted to get off quickly. This view would sometimes be justified in terms of bitter experience; a mother might have left quickly with perhaps the passing comment to staff, 'Oh, he'll be alright, he's been to playgroup', but the child may then have cried bitterly at being left so abruptly. The length of time that mothers were asked to stay varied. Some insisted on only 20 minutes or so, some for as much as several days.

Table 2.4: Degree to which mother is asked to stay on child's first day.

	Nursery (n = 171) %	Playgroup (n = 72) %
Yes, always	56	43
Only if the child seems upset	34	53
Not usually or never	10	4

In contrast, some nurseries encouraged mothers to bring their children and leave promptly. Although ostensibly a rather harsh procedure, once again it was often justified in terms of bitter experience. Like it or not, entry into nursery school or class does involve separation of child from mother and asking mothers to stay can simply prolong the agony for both. Many respondents mentioned that children would often appear desperately upset whilst their mothers' departure was *imminent*, thus putting mothers into a difficult and conflicting position, but once their mothers had gone they would in a matter of minutes be busily engaged in one aspect or another of the nursery scene. In only the rare case was a child reported to be continually upset once mother had gone.

These two systems are clearly opposed to each other but have in common the fact that they stem from a policy arrived at by staff. The other schools fell into a third category: the length of time a mother stays was largely left up to the mother, albeit in consultation with nursery staff. The justification sometimes expressed here was that mothers know their children's needs best and until staff know the child better it is advisable that she take the responsibility for decisions about separation. Usually staff remarked that they played it by ear and according to the individual child and circumstances. They would let things ride for a week or so and only then would they perhaps venture to suggest a mother might leave. One teacher let mothers stay as long as they liked because she did not feel she had the right to ask them to leave.

Mothers' views about how to approach separation also varied, according to nursery staff. Some were apparently very keen to get away from the nursery as soon as possible. This was variously attributed to mothers having a part-time job, wanting to get back to a younger sibling, or simply wanting to have time for her own pursuits. On the other hand some mothers were reported to find it very difficult to leave their child and unless it was suggested to them, might well stay indefinitely. What mothers actually felt about this is reported in Chapters 3 and 5.

Apart from the two main entry strategies – the staggered system and mothers staying on the first day – schools did not appear to have a well thought out policy with regard to helping children settle. The overriding response was that staff 'played it by ear' according to the individual child and circumstance. This is obviously an important consideration and it would not be possible to arrive at policies applicable to every situation. On the other hand we did detect a rather unprepared quality to staff's reactions, as if they responded to newcomers only *after* they observed a need for it – the most obvious case being when a child was upset. In very few cases was there evidence of a prepared strategy with newcomers, for example of ensuring that each was given attention and observed closely. In the light of our observations of children reported below, we consider this an important consideration for it is possible that staff may be too late in recognizing a child's negative but covert reaction.

5. The nursery and playgroup environments and how they differ from the home environment

Before we consider how children behave on entry we would like to consider what kind of environment – social and physical – the child will find in the nursery and playgroup.

The most obvious characteristics from the child's point of view will be the large number of children and the amount of equipment he will encounter, as well as the size of the premises. In nurseries there were on average 34 children per morning session and 33 per afternoon session. Large groups of children also produce a lot of noise and some staff identified this as a problem for newcomers to the nursery, observing that a child could appear bemused and a little frightened on his first days by the intensity of noise that surrounded him. And indeed one must sympathize with the child; although he may be used to the noise of television and radio within his home, and traffic outside it, the degree of noise created by about 40 children at full throttle in one room can be a daunting experience for anyone. One teacher remarked that to her mind 20 children were enough for a child to come to terms with; 40 was simply too many.

What is more, the number of adults available to the child – compared to what he will find in the home – has decreased. In the nursery sample, there was effectively one adult for every ten children. Many staff thought that having to share only a few adults with many other children was a key difference between home and nursery. From having a relatively intense relationship with his parents and other significant adults the child must now come to terms with a more impersonal and more thinly spread contact with adults. As one teacher said, 'children may have to share in the home, but it's not the same, they haven't got to share with 30 others'.

Apart from these basic characteristics, what kinds of experiences and organization will the child meet? Perhaps the best way of conveying a preliminary picture is to describe one morning routine as it was recounted to us by a nursery class teacher:

The children come in at 9–9.30 and we greet each child. We ask the children to bring a toy from their home – this is part of the routine. We consider it to be very important that the child brings something of the home into the nursery. Then the child is free to choose – we only limit the number of children who can play with the large bricks. There is always art activity out or the children can do painting. The children then go into the hall. A lot of these children come from flats and so we tend to let them rush around and let off steam. There is set-up apparatus but we tend to let them engage in imaginative play and it is therefore quite different from an infant session. Children then come back for milk. We have a kind of cafe situation where one child is given the job of waiter and about five other children at a time are served by the waiter. This is a social occasion and enables imaginative play. We find the children get used to this and get on with it without any adult supervision whatsoever. The others meanwhile engage in free play again. There is then a quiet activity, e.g. a story on the mat. On Mondays and Fridays the children watch TV upstairs. We used to take children to watch the television really in order to get them into the reception class where the television was located. The television has now been moved upstairs to a separate room but, although I'm not madly keen on children watching TV because they get quite enough at home, I still maintain two sessions per week. On Wednesday children have story. And on Tuesday and Thursday I bring the guitar in and sing songs with the children. At 11-11.30, and while the story is going on, mums come in and collect their children. I acknowledge that this could interrupt the story but I feel that the children usually know the story so well that it doesn't really matter.

This routine is not untypical. The usual mix was between free play with set out equipment, more staff-directed group events, and time spent outside – perhaps the nearest a child gets to really 'free' play.

Degree of structure in nursery and playgroup

One of the greatest differences between nurseries concerned the type of staff-directed sessions, as can be seen in Table 2.5. Most of the nurseries had

Table 2.5: Type of directed sessions per day (i.e. sessions for the whole class led by an adult) in nursery classes and schools.

	Everyday	3–4 day/wk	1–2 day/wk	Less than 1 day/wk	Never	N
	%	%	%	%	%	
Register	31	1	5	2	61	149
Milk	58	–	1	3	37	148
Story	77	4	5	3	12	157
TV	4	6	21	7	61	147
Radio	1	1	18	16	64	148
Music/sing-ing drama/ rhymes	62	18	11	2	7	148
Physical activities (e.g. games)	31	12	35	8	15	144

some kind of story and some form of music, singing, drama or rhyme period during the course of a session, but beyond that they varied. A minority made register a formal occasion, insisting that all children attend and respond to their names. As this usually occurred first thing in the morning or afternoon it could also serve to bring the children together for an introductory chat and invite conversation about home activities. More schools made milk a group occasion, again some attempting to create a setting for desultory conversation with the children. On the other hand only a slightly smaller number of schools preferred to have a more informal system where children helped themselves to milk when they felt like it. For both these types of sessions – register and milk – nurseries tended to polarize between those that had them as directed sessions every day and those who never structured them in this way.

Table 2.6 shows the number of directed sessions per day in the nursery sample. We were particularly interested in the type and extent of these because they are likely to be one key difference between home and nursery routines. In the majority of schools children experienced one or two such situations every day; in only two per cent of schools were no sessions directed by staff.

Table 2.6: Number of directed sessions per day (nursery classes and schools).

| | Number of sessions per day | | | | | |
	0	1	2	3	4	5
Number of nurseries	2	53	48	21	9	2
Percentage of nurseries	1	39	36	16	7	1

To some extent the type and degree of directed sessions will reflect staffs' views about the degree to which children's activities should be structured. Although a difficult distinction to make, Table 2.7 looks more directly at it because staff were asked to what extent they structured children's time in the nursery. It can be seen that the majority tended to use a system that was mainly unstructured but with some control of the activities pursued.

It was our impression from the interviews that the main emphasis was on a child-centred approach, though this was qualified in all cases by at least one directed session. Certainly no one articulated a consciously 'curriculum-centred' approach. The kind of approach we heard expressed was that the children were free to interact with any of the available equipment and staff would only direct proceedings if a child was being noisy or disruptive or in the case of new and complex activities like craft activities.

Table 2.7: Degree of structure in nursery.

	% (n = 148)
Mainly unstructured (activities may be set out but children are under no obligation to do them)	7
Mainly unstructured, but children are encouraged to do certain activities	66
Unstructured to some extent but children are required to pursue certain tasks or activities	26

Another approach to the same issue concerns the extent of control over individual activities. Table 2.8 shows results for both nurseries and playgroups.

Table 2.8: Degree of control over individual activities.

Certain individual activities and tasks are:	Per cent of Nurseries (n = 149)	Per cent of Playgroups (n = 71)
a) required of each child	17	4
b) encouraged generally	61	54
c) left to the choice of individual children	18	38
d) no policy	3	4

It can be seen that playgroup staff, more than nursery staff, tended to leave the choice of activities to the individual child.

Clearer evidence of differences in the degree of structure between nurseries and playgroups came from our question about whether children were taken for more formal sessions (e.g. pre-reading and number work, workbooks). Nurseries were much more likely to take these (79 per cent of nurseries took them as opposed to 6 per cent of playgroups). The number of children who took part was also larger – an average of eight as opposed to five. Of course one must also remember that nurseries also tend to take older children.

To sum up the discussion so far. Newcomers to the nursery and playgroup will have to adjust to a larger number of children spread between several adults, a large amount of noise and equipment, and some (though varying) degree of control over their activity, in particular concerning their participation in group sessions directed by staff.

Further differences between home and nursery

Other more qualitative differences also exist between home and nursery settings. One aspect mentioned by nursery teachers concerned the different behavioural demands in the nursery and home. This was expressed in various ways but the essential argument was that children were expected to comply with a more overt set of rules in the nursery than in the home. As one teacher said, 'There may be rules at home, but the rules are geared to the child, not to society'. This comment points to a key difference: the home tends to be personalized and particular to the child, whilst in the nursery the child is expected to behave in terms of group demands. One teacher expressed this rather formally, 'We have an expected level of compliance with authority'. Some were quick to point out that discipline in the nursery was not heavy handed: 'We insist on very few things really, but they're basic, e.g. not hurting each other, being quiet during story, not racing about, putting things away'.

Staff in the interview sample spoke in more detail of the home in terms of its influence on the child's 'educational' experiences. Many, for example, spoke of the lack of conversation and joint activities between child and parents and the way that this was reflected in speech problems at school. Many also mentioned the lack of meaningful stimulation in homes despite the expensive furnishing and clothes. The subject of television often arose. The feeling was that children were allowed to watch indiscriminately in order to keep them quiet and out of mischief.

Differences between home backgrounds

But staff also recognized that home circumstances varied. It was felt that children from flats, and especially those in high rise blocks, found the sheer size and freedom of the nursery quite overwhelming. Such children needed to let off steam, especially in outdoor play, in order to live out experiences bottled up at home.

Other, more qualitative, differences between homes were also identified. To return to the theme of the home as a 'learning' environment, in contrast to the picture painted above, some children were felt to experience a more formal educational pressure in the *home* than the nursery. Some parents were reported to be very concerned that the child learn to read and write at an early age and felt a little dissatisfied with the play approach to pre-reading and pre-number work. In the face of this situation the 'compensatory' model of nursery education was turned on its head: children were now allowed to let off steam and simply play together for its own sake in order to 'compensate' for the rather formal and rigid approach in the home. This highlights cultural differences in parental attitudes and expectations which it is known can influence scholastic progress (Douglas, 1964; Plowden Report, 1967). From the point of view of the present topic, it indicates the need for a sensitive consideration of a child's home experiences and the need to adapt the child's experiences accordingly; one approach may be appropriate to one child but a quite different approach may be required for another.

Coming as it does from school staff, this account of home life is biased no doubt, and it may be felt to reflect the distortions possible in 'professional' views on lay life. We have some bearing on this in the account of the parental interviews found in the next chapter. But before we leave this issue it might be worth mentioning that many staff also pointed to the distinguished place of the child's relationship with his parents and the value of home life. Most considered part-time preferable to full-time nursery education, because they felt children needed to establish a strong relationship with their mothers. One teacher also felt that the home had advantages from an educational point of view because of the more likely one-to-one relationship and greater sensitivity to the child's needs and level of competence that this allowed.

6. Children's reactions to entry

This will be explored more fully in Chapter 4, but we would like to first present the views of those working in nurseries and playgroups.

Degree of upset on entry

The majority of our respondents reported that only a few children showed obvious signs of being upset, e.g. crying or clinging to their mothers (see Table 2.9). Interestingly, staff in playgroups reported rather less cases of upset than those in nurseries. If this is an accurate picture then it tends to contradict the assumption we have often heard expressed, by both playgroup and nursery staff, that entry into playgroup is more traumatic for children. Some playgroup staff, for example, were a little aggrieved about nurseries because they felt it was the playgroup who had the nasty job of helping

Table 2.9: Degree of upset on entry.

	Nursery (n = 166)	Playgroup (n = 72)
Number of children upset:	%	%
None	1	–
Only one or two	69	85
Several	27	15
Many	4	–

children through their initial and often painful separation from their mothers – children who might later attend nursery classes or school. The fact that playgroups tend to take younger children adds to the contradiction for these might be expected to be more upset on separation. Whether the more informal atmosphere in playgroups helps, is an open question.

In some nursery situations the question of upset on entry was confounded in the sense that children had already taken part in sometimes several pre-visits and they had already adjusted to the nursery environment by the time of their official day of entry. It was no surprise that those interviewed in nurseries who organized pre-visits of this kind reported no signs of upset. On the other hand one nursery that did not organize pre-visits of any kind reported relatively excessive degrees of upset – in this case one-half the group of newcomers were reported to be upset.

Different types of reaction to entry

Everyone agreed that children respond in very different ways to the nursery. One common reaction was reported to be a fair degree of hesitancy. This is reflected in staying close to a parent at first but also in the child locating himself somewhere in the nursery, say at a table, and not moving for some time while watching proceedings. One teacher remarked that some children stand back like this for up to 20 minutes and perhaps longer.

Another almost opposite form of reaction is the child who enters the nursery environment in an excited fashion, flitting from one activity to another. Both types of reactions are obviously a reflection of the child's attempts to adjust to the new environment and one would assume that there is a reapproachment between the two reactions as the child adjusts, in the sense that the hesitant child will begin to try more activities and the excitable child will begin to spend more time at each activity. Several teachers, however, remarked that the latter type of reaction could lead to more serious long-term reactions. That is, after a period of say a few days, the excited child could react and not want to come anymore. One nursery nurse remarked, 'I prefer them to be upset at first and then get over it. If they come in all excited you always get a reaction.'

But a withdrawn reaction on entry can also lead to serious consequences if not watched closely. As one person said, 'the worst thing is quiet distress – those without tears. The kickers and screamers you can cope with but inward distress is the worst.' Understandably staff feel more able to cope with an overt reaction from children, no matter how negative. In such cases they can gauge a child's behaviour in the context of his circumstances and more clearly see how they might help him. The withdrawn child is, however, something of a mystery and perhaps a threat, and what behaviour to adopt toward him is not easily specified. The problems involved became evident to us during our own observations of children's entry into a nursery unit. One particular child was quiet and unforthcoming but because he was not obviously upset, like the one or two children who cried, he was mostly left to find his own activities and acquaintances. Although apparently quite content, close observation indicated that he was rather aloof from the other children and did not appear to easily approach adults for direction. The other children did not appear to notice him and once or twice his rather clumsy attempts to initiate a game with another child received a neutral response. After three sessions in the nursery his mother came to collect him as usual and, on sight of her, he burst into tears. The child has apparently never returned. The moral of the story as we see it, is that staff must keep a close eye on all the newcomers and not just those who are obviously upset, because the unobtrusive reaction may mask a great insecurity that equally requires reassurance and direction from staff.

Another reaction, mentioned by some, was the development of an attachment by the child with one of the nursery staff, usually a nursery nurse. Invariably this replacement attachment was not discouraged by staff for they seemed to feel that it would help the child in the short term and the child would soon outgrow it.

Which aspects of the nursery were most difficult for children?

We asked questions concerning those aspects of the nursery to which children found it difficult to adjust. Our interview respondents felt that children were least happy in group situations involving story time, singing, etc., finding it very difficult to settle and attend to the topic at hand. Although many teachers blamed this on the lack of such activities in the home, it is as well to remember the limits on children's understanding at this age and the fact that appropriate behaviour in groups is an acquired skill that young children may not have had any reason to acquire at an earlier stage. During our own observations of newcomers in group situations we noticed that they could be unaware of even such basic skills as recognizing that the group had a leader (a member of staff) whose instructions were to be followed. These skills are central to many situations children will encounter later in their school life – situations within which academic instruction takes place – and it is appropriate that staff should be concerned about children's acquisition of them. It might be added from our own observations that children can be left to clarify for themselves what is expected of them and sometimes they can arrive at rather inappropriate conclusions, e.g. concerning how to behave in story and singing sessions, that then have to be commented on.

Other difficulties encountered by children were also mentioned. Several mentioned the fears of some children in nursery classes or units when they have to leave the new found security of the nursery for the school corridor or hall. It is the sheer vastness of these, and the fact that children do not know where they are being led, which causes problems and brings them close to staff's sides.

Similar problems were also mentioned with regard to milk. In actual fact the ostensibly simple task of drinking milk out of a bottle involves a surprisingly complex series of motor and possibly social coordinations, not helped in many cases by elaborate rituals which often take place. For example, in one nursery class, children had to find their personal name tag, put it on a bottle in a crate, come back at a later point after washing their hands, locate the appropriate bottle, take a straw, push the straw through the bottle top, go to a certain part of the nursery, attempt to suck out of the straw and not tilt the bottle, take the top off the bottle and put it into an appropriate bin, put the straw in another bin, put the bottle back into the crate, decide whether to have a slice of fruit or not and, if they survived the course, return to their previous activity! In fact the nursery nurses in this nursery anticipated the problems that newcomers would face in learning all these steps. Because of the clear and sensitive way that the ritual was explained it represented a problem task that children soon found pleasure in mastering, and, moreover, found pleasure in helping other children with.

Further questions about children's behaviour on entry, e.g. their toy preferences, sex differences and associations with previous experiences, we will reserve until Chapter 4. We would like now to discuss answers we received concerning more general questions about children's behaviour.

Settling into the nursery

The first of these concerns 'settling' into the nursery. Table 2.10 presents the length of time staff felt it took children to settle in nurseries and playgroups.

Table 2.10: Length of time it takes children to settle.

	Nursery (n = 156) %	Playgroup (n = 72) %
Less than one week	14	21
Up to two weeks	33	36
Up to three weeks	26	31
Up to one month	11	13
Over one month	17	–

In both nurseries and playgroups it was felt that the bulk of newcomers had settled by their third week though rather more newcomers took longer to settle in nurseries. This may owe much, of course, to rather greater demands on children in the nursery compared with the home (see above) and the playgroup. It may also owe something to the way the term 'settled' is used and understood. It is clearly a broad term and we asked our respondents to clarify what it meant for them. Answers from nursery staff varied to some extent but involved concepts like being happy, being able to part easily from mother, being able to concentrate on an activity and not flit from one to another, voluntarily approaching and talking to staff, forming relationships with other children and contributing to group activities. Playgroup staff saw settled behaviour in much the same way, though they placed most emphasis on 'mixing freely with others' as a criterion of being settled.

It can be seen that definitions of 'settled' behaviour covered a lot of ground. Perhaps the most central theme was the move, on the child's part, toward self-reliance and independence. In terms of the child's overall development the beginning of independence from his parents is one of the most crucial stages in his life and one of the most important functions of the nursery. It is also crucial for development more narrowly defined in terms of factors associated with education, because children are unlikely to profit from any educational setting without some degree of prior independence and stability. Some staff held this notion of independence as a conscious policy, for others it seemed to be an assumption underlying more practical concerns.

Without wishing to denigrate this aim, we were struck in some cases by the way in which an 'independent' child seemed to be measured in terms of his unobtrusiveness, rather in the way that a 'good' child is measured by some parents in terms of his passivity and compliance with requests. We did get the feeling from some staff that settled behaviour could be equated with the child not bothering them or causing disruptions in the nursery.

We also asked staff about behaviours they considered indicative of an 'unsettled' child. Logically enough, most mentioned the behaviour patterns converse to those mentioned for settled behaviour. Unsettled children are those who can not concentrate on an activity for any length of time, those who are destructive, do not form relationships with other children or staff, and cannot accept the nursery routine.

Interestingly, several respondents mentioned that some children find it easier to relate to other children than staff. One head gave an extreme example of a little girl whose mother and father often quarrelled. After one particularly violent encounter the little girl was later found hiding in the garden shed and from that moment on would not talk to anyone. After entry into nursery class, however, she had begun to relate, and converse with, some other children and the head felt it would not be long before she would begin to relate to staff. Other examples were less extreme but did indicate that some children find it easier to interact with other children than adults. It is tempting to speculate why this may be the case. Perhaps it is because other children are at a similar level of competence and their behaviour is therefore easily grasped and a response easily made; or perhaps through experiences at home children have come to perceive adults only as custodians and not as stimulating companions. But whatever the reason, several respondents have mentioned the unique character of child-child interaction, and how much they would like to know more about what children actually said to each other as they pursued some activity together. Before we leave this point, it must also be said that becoming a member of a strange group of children can be difficult and some children were found to more easily relate to *adults* than other children. This was especially the case with only children from home backgrounds where a child already experienced incentives toward educational achievement.

Definitions of settled and unsettled behaviour can therefore vary from one child to another but definitions will also differ in terms of respondents' aims for pre-school education – some may value social relationships, others conceptual attainments – and children's behaviour will be assessed accordingly. Identification of settled behaviour is also relative to a child's age and expectations based on that. In a sense a child can never be settled as such, because at some point he or she must move on to the next educational stage and different expectations and definitions will then prevail. From this point of view becoming 'settled' is not an absolute phenomenon but a relative one and it is possible that it will more likely take a 'curvilinear' than a 'linear' trend with age. In other words a child may come to fulfil the expectations made on him by the nursery – he will use activities constructively and make relationships – but by the end of his life in the nursery he may again be unsettled as he realizes, albeit dimly, that new expectations and a new life will soon confront him. The most obvious example of this concerns 'rising fives' who have become a little bored at the usual nursery routine and equipment available and now search for something more demanding.

7. Parental involvement after entry

In Chapter 1 we argued that transition is best conceived as a process that extends beyond the immediate point of entry. An important part of this process will be contacts between parents and nursery during the child's time in the nursery. In this section we will look at this from the point of view of pre-school staff. Chapter 6 will take up parents' views.

Collecting children

There are several ways that parents come into contact with the nursery. The most basic occurs when parents bring and collect their child. This will happen in the case of virtually all parents because most schools insist that an adult known to the child bring and pick him up. Several staff explicitly said that for safety reasons they would not let an older brother or sister take the child home. For most schools the contacts that occurred at the beginning and the end of the session constituted the main form of contact between staff and parents. Virtually all remarked that this relatively extensive degree of informal contact did away with the need for more formally arranged visits (73 per cent of nursery classes and schools). Parents could discuss any problems or comments they might have and staff could in turn make their own comments. In comparison with later age levels this arrangement does allow a far more spontaneous and extensive degree of parental contact. Our main reservation would be the perennial problem that a more informal contact will tend to be taken up by some and not others. Several staff mentioned that some mothers would stay and chat for some time but that others would 'dump and run', as it were. The danger is that some mothers, for whatever reasons, may avoid contact with staff and problems may go unresolved. Another problem of concentrating all contacts at the beginning and the end of sessions is that some mothers may feel unhappy about discussing delicate matters whilst other mothers are around. It is also possible that staff, either because of lack of time, embarrassment, or possibly barriers brought about by their 'professional' status, will also find it difficult to talk to parents on an informal basis.

Formal contacts

Very few schools had a formal system of contacts with parents, e.g. interviews on a regular basis. Most had these only if problems arose. In the case of nursery classes or units attached to a main first or primary school, it was often the case that the nursery parents were invited to the main school events, e.g. open days, and thus there was less inclination to provide separate events in the nursery. However, we did get the impression that there was relatively little response from nursery parents to main school events. One school, for example, organized so called family assemblies, but, although welcome to come, only four or five nursery mothers did so. There was a relatively higher response to open events specific to the nursery. Eighty-four per cent of nurseries held open days and other events for parents and of these over 50 per cent reported that more than 50 per cent of mothers attended.

Schools differed in terms of whether they preferred a day or evening setting for the open event. Although the day event may be more practical, several staff did recognize that this tended to stop fathers coming and so were prepared to put themselves out in order to encompass this usual stranger to the nursery. Even so, the number of fathers who did attend was generally reported to be far lower than mothers for talks or open days, either during the day or evening; under ten per cent of fathers usually attended. One head also made the important point that parents could not get a true picture of what the nursery was like from an evening visit. There would be no children, all the apparatus would be tidied away and staff would be on their best, but not necessarily their most usual, behaviour. For some parents these visits may afford their longest and most detailed experience of the nursery environment and this head preferred parents to experience the nursery as it normally occurred.

Some schools provided a more focussed event for parents of nursery children. A few, for example, put on talks or films involving a topical issue. In one school the policy was to encourage parents to supply a topic of interest and the school would then organize a discussion on it, led by a local 'expert' in the field. Another went one better and showed a film on the topic and followed this by a talk chaired by, say, a health visitor. The obvious drawback to staging these events is the worry that many schools would have about the degree of parental response. Staff might not be happy about arranging a film or speaker for an audience of less than half a dozen parents. Surprisingly, we could not detect a clear regional or socioeconomic class influence; some schools from predominantly urban, working class council estates had a high degree of parental interest and support. We did get the impression that lack of parental support had more to do with school expectations of, and relationships with, parents. To some staff, parental lack of interest was an assumption which they seemed to do little to test out.

Parents spending time in the nursery

But there are obviously limits to how much parents can become involved in school through the medium of essentially extracurricular activities. A number of schools are now attempting to meet this challenge by inviting parents to spend time in the nursery. It must be noted that opinions amongst our nursery respondents were not at one on this aim. Some schools as a matter of policy positively encouraged parents to stay for as long as they liked (41 per cent). But at the other extreme some staff did not at all like the idea of parents sitting in on a session (21 per cent). One teacher expressed herself thus: 'Unless they have a particular talent, I'm not keen on it. It's a liability otherwise. Really, I'm adequately staffed and don't need any extra help. In any case not many would come forward.' Another teacher thought that the nursery environment was too small to conveniently house extra adults. And another teacher embraced fully the ideal of parental involvement in the nursery but found parents so demanding on her time – some were very distressed – that her relationship with the children suffered. Midway between these two attitudes were those who encouraged help in some cases (38 per cent). Some of these, one felt, had been carried along in the move toward greater parental involvement but appeared to have little commitment to it and appeared quite content with only a few regular attenders.

What then of the extent of parental involvement in nurseries where this was acceptable? Everyone stressed that not all mothers were as willing as others to come. Well over half the nurseries who encouraged mothers to help said that less than ten per cent of mothers actually did help. Some schools adopted a rota system which might involve a list of dates on a notice board and an invitation to parents to put their name down at a time convenient to them (10 per cent). Usually however, only a minority volunteered. Some adopted a very flexible rota system (21 per cent). But most had given up the rota idea altogether and accepted the fact that only five or six mothers would attend regularly (69 per cent). Reasons given by staff for why mothers would not come included having a job – though this was rare – and having another, younger, child at home. It was accepted that some mothers were also very keen to get some time to themselves away from their child. Some respondents were quick to express their sympathy with this; parental involvement in school life may be a commendable aim but mothering is also a demanding task and a rest from it may be valuable from the mother's point of view. In some cases there were cultural pressures which mitigated against parental involvement. In one Asian community, one dwelling often housed an extended family and it was the expectation of (especially) the grandparents that their daughter would return home after delivering her child to school.

Several respondents mentioned that they preferred the child to become settled into the nursery before they asked mothers to spend time there. The reason for this is that the growth in independence of children from their parents would be hindered by introducing mothers into the nursery with this delicate process not yet resolved.

There was no clear cut pattern about what staff preferred mothers to do in the nursery. Several mentioned that they adjusted this to the individual mother – if she looked in need of direction then she was given a job to do. Any hidden talents that might come to the fore were also quickly harnessed and these skills deployed. Sometimes this deployment could be misplaced as in the case of one mother, thought to be a capable cook, who put trays of biscuits in the oven and forgot to take them out. Apparently she had taken to heart staff's comment that, from the child's point of view, the preparation was all important – never mind the finished product! Many staff were quick to point out that parents were not really aids in the nursery; if anything, the main benefit was to the mother.

We asked staff about the effect a mother's presence might have on her child. As one might expect, children were reported to react to this by showing off, staying close to their mother or not letting another child interact with her. But in no case did this seem an insurmountable problem and children were unlikely to react in this way for very long. This kind of reaction could also be tempered by staff intervention – involving mothers elsewhere with a job, for example.

Considering the claims often made for greater parental involvement in playgroups, it is interesting to compare them on the same dimensions. Rather more playgroups than nurseries encouraged mothers to help as a matter of policy (63 per cent as opposed to 41 per cent), though there were still some who discouraged help (13 per cent compared to 21 per cent). There was a much higher percentage of mothers who did help – well over half the playgroups who did ask for help received it from more than 26 per cent of mothers. This type of help was more likely to be organized on a rota basis (34 per cent strict rota, 40 per cent flexible rota). Playgroups and nurseries were about even in the extent to which they encouraged fathers to help in the nursery.

Throughout this section the emphasis has always been on mothers. This is not simply convenience of usage – it does reflect a dearth of father involvement in nursery or playgroup life. Virtually no fathers were reported to spend time in the nursery though a larger percentage did bring or collect their child. The reason for this is obviously largely attributable to employment demands, though there was also reported to be a resistance from fathers. Yet the cases we did encounter of men helping in the nursery were a great success. We did hear it said that fathers, more than mothers, need a definite job to focus on and we ourselves observed a father leading an enthralled group engaged in woodwork. Several schools also invited fathers along to talk about their professions. One problem here is that some jobs are not easily communicated to pre-school children. Policemen, firemen and bus conductors are tangible enough but many white collar occupations might well be incomprehensible. (The present writers remember with some embarrassment the difficulties they have faced in explaining to pre-school and even much older children what their job entails whilst engaged in classroom observations!) Even so, one head described how surprised she was to observe the attentiveness of children to a town planner talking about his job.

Involvement of parents in pre-school life is a complex issue, with many intricacies, and it has been possible to only touch on several aspects of it here. For the moment we can say that this ideal has by no means been fully embraced by nursery staff. Many parents, for their part, still feel uneasy about spending time in school. One enormous difficulty is that the 'professional' status of nursery staff is not easily accompanied by an equal partnership with parents. We suspect that much of the failure of parental involvement in some schools rests on this divisive role relationship, which may underlie lip service to parental involvement. Once again there is no universal panacea and each school will have to arrive at its own definition and approach. It seems pretty clear from our respondents' answers that PTAs and other parent associations are not the answer. Only a small fraction of schools had them and most had either never formed one or had given them up. They aroused widespread reservations and dissatisfaction.

Despite these difficulties it seems clear that one of the biggest challenges of early child education is to more fully come to terms with a greater cooperation with parents. If a positive relationship can be set up at an early age in a child's school life then, in the light of the ever decreasing contact between parents and school as the child ages, initial attitudes need not set the scene and become entrenched through want of conflicting experience to the contrary. At very least some attempt should be made to counter the negative attitude some parents have toward school and school staff, based on their own school experiences. It seems likely that this, and the confusion that many parents feel about modern teaching methods, can only be countered by staff encouragement, and experience of what actually goes on in classrooms.

8. Contacts between playgroups and nurseries, and between both and primary schools

One of the messier aspects of early transition, at least from a researcher's point of view, if not from the child's, is that children can move from one pre-school setting to another before they reach primary school. A sizeable minority of children, for example, move from playgroup into nursery classes or schools. Thirty-four per cent of our nursery sample reported that more than 26 per cent of their children came from playgroups. What then of the contacts between these two settings?

Only a minority of playgroups (32 per cent) said they had any contacts with nursery schools or classes. Of these the most popular type of contact was reported to be a visit to the nursery, the next in frequency being a visit from the nursery teacher to the playgroup. In a similar vein, of those playgroups who did not have contacts but wished them to take place, the most popular contact required was a visit to the nursery so that children could be prepared for it.

In some areas, of course, there will be no scope for contact because there may not be a nursery nearby. This is not the whole story however because of those playgroups who did not have contacts, 61 per cent said that they did not want them. This touches on a sore point in the pre-school field. Although we met only the rare case of outright resentment we did meet a fair degree of caution between staff in the two settings. Some nursery personnel felt threatened by what they saw as the rise of amateurs, whom they saw being widely supported as a low cost provision in an economic recession. For their part some playgroup staff felt nursery people hid behind a wall of professionalism and were even misguided about what activities were provided for children. Often the views of each other were tolerant enough but stereotypes were expressed. Several playgroup people, for example, were horrified because they thought that children at nursery schools and classes were forced to sit down to formal sessions. Some nursery people on the other hand had an idea that children in all playgroups were free to dash around without any guidance from adults whatsoever. Obviously these stereotypes are born and fostered by an ignorance of what actually goes on in the other setting. The depressing thing from this point of view is that so few staff seemed inclined to find out what went on.

We asked questions, of both nurseries and playgroups, concerning what they saw as the essential differences between the two settings. For their part nursery staff stressed the fact they were trained staff and that the activities provided some degree of planning and structure behind them. Playgroups on the other hand tended to stress that they were more informal and facilitated more parental involvement.

To get a more strictly comparable picture of the different attitudes and aims in the two settings we also asked staff from both to complete a so-called 'reasons grid'; adapted from one used by Sheila Shinman (1975). This was a set of 15 reasons for desiring pre-school attendance and we asked respondents to rate each reason in terms of its importance on a five point scale.

Table 2.11: **Differences between nursery and playgroup staffs' reasons for desiring pre-school attendance. Mean scores**[1]

Reason	Playgroup staff		Nursery school/class staff		Differences[2] between views of nursery and playgroup statistically
	means	ranks	means	ranks	significant?
1) Enabling mothers to understand their children	2.47	13	2.12	12	yes
2) Enabling a child to learn through play	1.13	2	1.19	2	
3) Preparation for later school life	1.63	9	1.79	10	
4) Enabling a child to contact other adults	2.23	12	1.99	11	
5) Enabling a child to talk and listen and develop intellectual skills	1.41	6	1.14	1	yes
6) Enabling a child to develop coordination, balance and other physical skills	1.47	7	1.36	6	

7) Enabling a child to contact other children	1.11	1	1.27	3	
8) Enabling a child to be more independent	1.36	5	1.34	5	
9) Enabling mothers to have more time to themselves and their own activities	3.03	15	3.65	15	yes
10) Enabling a child to become part of a group	1.52	8	1.73	9	
11) Enabling mothers to meet and get advice from staff	2.60	14	2.35	13	
12) Enabling a child to engage in activities he couldn't easily do at home, e.g. messy play or use of apparatus, like climbing frames	1.22	4	1.60	7	yes
13) Enabling a child to learn how to share and behave with other children	1.16	3	1.33	4	
14) Enabling mothers to make friends with other mothers	2.17	11	2.81	14	yes
15) Enabling a child to gain a lasting educational advantage	2.16	10	1.67	8	yes

[1] Scores on each item ranged from 1–5, 1 being the most important, 5 the least important. Therefore the higher the mean score the least important an item on the grid was thought to be.

[2] See Appendix 1 for details of statistical analyses and results.

There was a fair degree of agreement between the two groups (see Table 2.11). When the averaged scores for each reason were ranked from those given the highest priority (1) to those given the lowest (15), on only three reasons did the ranks differ by more than two positions (reasons 5, 12, 14). Both teachers and playgroup leaders considered the benefits to mothers, of pre-school attendance for their children (reasons 1, 9, 11, 14), to be of relatively little importance. 'Enabling mothers to have more time to themselves and their own activities' was considered to be the least important of all reasons by both nursery and playgroup staff. (We shall see in the next chapter that mothers, when given the same 'reasons grid', also put a low priority on benefits to themselves.)

There were some differences in emphasis, however, and these were most marked in the kinds of benefits pre-school attendance was seen to have for children. Of all the reasons for children attending pre-school, nursery school and class staff ranked the most obviously 'educational' reason first ('enabling a child to talk and listen and develop intellectual skills'). Playgroup staff on the other hand ranked this reason fifth, putting the more social and general reason – 'enabling a child to contact other children' – first. Nursery staff, consistent with these results, as well as their training, also considered pre-school more likely 'to enable a child to gain a lasting educational advantage'.

As well as the social reasons, playgroup staff placed a higher priority on 'enabling a child to engage in activities he would not easily do at home'.

Nursery staff, therefore, saw pre-school experience more in terms of its benefits for intellectual development and educational progress (at least in terms of the 'grid' they were asked to complete), while playgroup staff, though agreeing in other respects, tended to identify the more social and practical advantages to the child.

Work such as this goes some way toward clarifying exact differences in the aims and approaches in the two settings. There seems little alternative in the present situation to the continued parallel existence of both nurseries and playgroups for some time to come and the more staff in each setting under-stand what goes on in the other, and clarify what the particular values and roles of each might be, the healthier will be the pre-school scene in Britain.

We will only mention in passing contacts between playgroups and nurser-ies on the one hand and primary schools on the other because this is the subject of another NFER report (Cleave, Jowett and Bate, 1982). The large majority of nurseries said they had contacts with primary schools (95 per cent), the most frequent form of contact being a visit to the teacher and classroom that the child would go into. The same situation pertained for playgroups, though the frequencies were not so high. The majority of nursery and playgroup staff said they were reasonably happy about the contacts they had with primary school. One way in which the playgroup/infant school link appeared to fall down was with regard to passing on information about children. Whereas 95 per cent of nurseries passed on information, 86 per cent of playgroups did not.

There was a clear distinction between nursery schools on the one hand and nursery classes and units on the other. The main difference stems from the fact that nursery schools are housed in separate buildings, usually some distance from the nearest primary school, whilst nursery classes and units are at least in the same grounds. It is also difficult for nursery schools to establish a close link with primary schools because their children tend to disperse to a number of them.

There can be little doubt, therefore, that the situation ought to be more favourable, from the point of view of transition, in the case of children moving from a nursery class or unit to an attached primary school. There are several other advantages. Because of the close proximity, children in the nursery will almost inevitably come into contact with the primary school. For example, the nursery may be approached by an area or corridor common to other parts of the school, or the nursery playground may be adjacent to the main school playground. This means that children will have achieved a fair degree of familiarity with the main school environment prior to their first days in a reception class.

Another advantage concerns the potential correspondence between nursery and infant staff about children who move up to infant school. In fact although 95 per cent of nurseries said they passed on information to primary schools, we did not find a very coherent system of record keeping. Some schools had evolved quite elaborate checklists, mini-tests or written reports on children, while others appeared reluctant to pin children down in this way. This means that there has to be a heavy reliance on oral accounts, at least in some nurseries, in order that detailed information be passed on one child. It is obviously far easier for this to occur in the case of an attached unit – staff may meet, for example, at lunch and points can be discussed as they come up. Ideally, this should allow an ongoing dialogue about children to take place.

Even so, schools did vary in the extent to which they capitalized on advantages of proximity. Some made conscious attempts to include nursery children in main school events, e.g. getting them to attend school assemblies and shows, and visit the class they would attend. In some schools, on the other hand, there appeared to be little attempt at integration; the attitude appeared to be that the fact of proximity was enough to ensure integration. But proximity is not enough and we did visit some nursery classes and units that were relatively isolated from main school life. This can be exacerbated in the case of nursery units that are physically detached from the main school for without conscious attempts to create links between the two, the nursery can be as effectively isolated as a nursery school on a separate site. This can affect staff as well as children and we did encounter resentment on the part of some nursery staff at what they felt was neglect by the rest of the school. For one head the isolation stemmed from the reticence of other teachers in the school to take on interest in or familiarize themselves with the nursery. Some nursery staff complained that main school staff tended not to be interested in receiving information on children, and return visits by children, once they had left the nursery, were not encouraged.

8. Summary

In this chapter a number of general issues concerning children's transition from home into nursery class, school and playgroup have been discussed. The chapter was based on questionnaires returned by staff in nursery classes and schools, and also by playgroup staff. A number of the nursery staff were also interviewed.

The chapter charted the course of a child entering pre-school. The very first contacts with pre-school prior to entry were described. Differences between pre-schools in the age at which children's names were put down on a waiting list were identified, as were different types of 'entrant'.

Visits by child and parents to the nursery prior to entry are of importance because they can set the seal on future parental involvement in children's lives in the nursery. The type and extent of visits varied from the cursory to those that were carefully organized, involving talks with staff and visits to the nursery. Some nursery staff are now also visiting parents and child in their own home, arguing that this can create a more relaxed and informed relationship with them.

Most pre-schools collected information on children prior to entry in an informal fashion, recording information as and when it came up and not having a deliberate policy. Contacts with other agencies, e.g. health visitors, doctors and social workers, can also be important in helping staff obtain a reliable picture of children, yet contacts were sometimes unsatisfactory and sometimes made difficult by rather unnecessary barriers between the different professions.

Attention was next turned to the day of entry itself and the procedures adopted by staff to help children settle. The two most common strategies were staggered entry and allowing parents to stay with children. Once again nurseries differed in both extent and type. Overall, though, staff in nurseries did not seem to have a deliberate policy and attended to newcomers after they observed a need for it. One danger of this essentially responsive attitude concerns children whose distress is not overtly expressed and whose problems might be discovered late by staff.

Differences between home, nursery and playgroup environments were then discussed. In nurseries children encountered more children, equipment and noise, though proportionately less adults. Differences in expectations and degree of structure were also identified.

Children react in different ways to entry and these, along with those aspects of the nursery children found most difficult, were assessed. Also discussed was the difficult problem of defining what constitutes 'settled' and 'unsettled' behaviour.

An important aspect of transition into pre-school concerns relationships between parents and staff after entry. The majority of contacts are inevitably informal, occurring for the most part at the beginning and end of sessions. Reluctance on the part of staff and parents may mean that little contact does take place. More formal types of contact, e.g. open days and talks, were discussed, as were the attitudes of staff in nurseries and playgroups to parents helping during a session. Staff seemed to have sympathy with the notion of parental involvement but practical efforts to set up such links were less obvious.

We encountered a fair degree of caution between staff in nurseries and playgroups and some views arose out of ignorance of what actually went on in the other setting. The views of staff in the two types of provision were compared on a 15 item 'grid'; nursery staff were orientated toward educational concerns, whilst playgroup staff saw more practical and social reasons for attending pre-school.

Finally, there was a brief discussion of contacts between nurseries and playgroups on the one hand and infant schools on the other. Nursery units attached to infant schools were most favourably situated with regard to transition but could be as effectively isolated as schools on separate sites.

Having looked in general at the process of transition from nursery and playgroup staff's point of view, we now turn to parents' perspectives on transition.

CHAPTER 3

Parent Interviews Prior to Entry

The home and family are of paramount importance as sources for the young child's experiences and in helping to shape development. Numerous studies have indicated, and common sense dictates, that the influence of home is pervasive and persistent throughout our life span. Moreover this influence is perhaps at its strongest during the first few years of life – years when the young child develops rapidly in all senses. An adequate and up to date picture of the home environment, the experiences and pattern of activities followed by two-and-a-half to three-year-olds was, therefore, considered essential in order to place the child's experience of entering pre-school into perspective. The interviews with parents were intended to achieve this aim. The interviews were also to provide information on the extent of parents' knowledge or belief about pre-school provision, the parents' reasons for wanting their children to attend or not as the case may be, the type of pre-school experience parents would choose, and the contacts they would like prior to and following their child's entry.

The reader is advised that throughout the following description of the sample and in presentation of findings the word 'parent' is interchangeable with 'mother' unless stated otherwise. This is because, with one exception, it was the mother who answered the majority of questions even when both parents were present. When fathers were present they were asked for their response to those questions specifically relating to them.

Following an outline of the way in which the sample was obtained and interviewed, the chapter presents the results of the interviews under five main headings.

1. Family background and home environment;
2. the pattern of children's daily lives and experience prior to nursery or playgroup entry;
3. parental attitudes to learning;
4. pre-school provision: parents' knowledge and choice of setting;
5. contact desired with pre-school before entry and anticipated reactions of parent and child.

The sample

Our original intention was to obtain around a hundred interviews. In the event eighty-six parents representing forty-three each of boys and girls (a purely fortuitous split) agreed to take part in the project. Budget constrictions led us to concentrate on two of the local authority areas used for the survey of nurseries and playgroups which were within daily travelling distance of our one interviewer. The plan was for a nursery from each area to be subsequently used for an intensive study of children as they entered (see next chapter).

For one area, through the cooperation of the area health authority we obtained a list of sixty-nine names and addresses of children born between June and August 1976. The children were therefore aged between two-and-a-half and three-years-old by the time their parents were interviewed in the spring of 1979. Health visitors agreed to contact as many of these parents as possible to prepare them for our visits. We then sent a letter asking for parents' cooperation and stating our intention to call on them and arrange a convenient time for the interview to take place. Fifty parents were interviewed in this way; of the nineteen remaining, six families had moved and could not be traced, and there were six refusals and seven non-contacts.

In addition to this sample, the head teachers of the two nursery schools designated for the observational study provided access to their lists of new intakes. Letters were sent to these parents explaining the purpose of the project and giving notice of a visit to arrange interviews. The schools approved the form of the letter and also agreed to answer parents' inquiries if this became necessary. Using this method thirty-six parents were interviewed in all; twenty-six in Area B prior to the autumn term of 1979 when their children were due to enter the nursery, and ten from Area A, prior to the spring term 1980. The shortfall between the number of parents interviewed having children due to start at these two nurseries (36) and the number of children subsequently observed (33, see Chapter 4) was due to the fact that three children, whose parents were interviewed, did not subsequently attend nursery class.

The sample was not therefore strictly a random one in the sense that the non-contacts may have had different views and the additional nursery sample were selected because they intended to send their children to nursery class. On the other hand there is little one can do about non-respondents and we will see below that the sample seemed to cover a range of backgrounds and views.

The interview

Each parent was interviewed using an interview schedule requiring answers to over a hundred questions. The interview elicited basic factual information on the physical and economic environment of the home, the children's daily routine, toy play and experiences; the parents' attitudes to learning; parents' involvement with their children, and parents' knowledge and desires regarding pre-school provisions. The schedule provided space for the interviewer to record answers in longhand which were later transferred to a coding grid.

The schedule took an hour on average to administer. The parents were generally welcoming, frequently offered tea or coffee, and seemed to appreciate the chance to discuss their young children's lives, past, present and future. A newsletter was left after the interview and mothers with children entering the nurseries were asked if they would cooperate in a further short interview towards the end of the children's first term.

1. Family background and home environment

Although the sample was not large we were attempting to reach families living in diverse social and economic circumstance in order to obtain a spectrum of descriptions of young children's lives in southern England urban areas. Of those in work, 41 per cent of the fathers had non-manual employment while 59 per cent were in skilled, semi-skilled manual work and unskilled occupations. This compares favourably with national breakdowns of employment categories where 40 per cent of the male working population are in the non-manual socioeconomic groups while 60 per cent fall into manual groups.[1] A breakdown of the sample is given in Table 3.1

Table   3.1: Socioeconomic   group   of
fathers in employment.

	Socioeconomic Group	Percentages
I	Professional, managerial	1
II	Intermediate non-manual	29
III	Skilled non-manual	11
	Total non-manual	41 (n = 33)
IV	Skilled manual	47
V	Semi-skilled manual	9
VI	Unskilled manual	3
	Total manual	59 (n = 46)

When this is compared with the latest available government statistics, our sample is seen to be slightly weighted towards the intermediate socioeconomic groups and skilled manual group while it under-represents those in

---

[1] From C.S.O., *Social Trends*, 1980 Edition, p. 125, HMSO.

'other' non-manual groups and those in semi-skilled and unskilled occupations. Only two of the fathers were unemployed and this was unrepresentative of the level of unemployment, which stood at around eight per cent during the time of the survey, though was somewhat lower than this in the areas covered in the survey. Of the eighty-six mothers, 64 per cent were housewives; eight per cent worked outside the home in full-time paid employment while ten per cent worked part-time during the day. A further 13 per cent worked during the evening or night mainly at part-time cleaning jobs and the remainder worked occasionally or took work into their homes. Approximately 30 per cent of our mothers therefore worked regularly. The 1978 official figure was just over 20 per cent of working mothers having children under three years of age. The higher percentage found in our survey probably reflects the opportunities for work in the particular areas of our survey and the gradual trends towards an increasing proportion of mothers with children under five entering employment. Five families were fatherless (six per cent). There were no motherless families in the sample. The current national estimate is that one-parent families with dependent children represent 11 per cent of all families with dependent children in Britain.

In terms of family composition the sample represented a wide range. The majority of families (58 per cent) had two children while a further 21 per cent were single child families. There were 12 per cent three-child, five per cent four-child and five per cent five-child families. Most of the families lived alone (94 per cent), five per cent had other family members living with them, while one single parent lived with her parents.

Physical environment

The physical environment in which the sample of children and their families lived varied greatly. Semi-detached or end of terrace and terraced housing accounted for 62 per cent and 26 per cent lived in maisonettes or flats, the latter being more often in tower blocks than houses or low-rise buildings. Most of the children (87 per cent) had homes with a garden or other outside space and 81 per cent of these were allowed unsupervised access to these. Most of the children played with tricycles or other large toys when outdoors. Nearly half were able to play with sand or water – usually water – when in the garden or enjoyed digging holes with spoons or spades.

Forty per cent of parents said that one or two rooms, excluding bathrooms and lavatories, in the home were prohibited areas to the child. The reasons given for this were usually connected with safety: to prevent the child making a mess or injuring himself. For example, one mother said she did not like the child going into her bedroom as she was afraid he would open her bottles and jars; another that her husband kept his carpentry tools in one room and the child was not allowed near these. Occasionally a room in the home was used as an office by one or other parent and children were usually kept out of such rooms. Only 16 per cent of families said they had provided their children with a playroom of their own and this more often than not was also their bedroom. It might seem that the remaining 60 per cent of children had a free run of the house, but in practice, this was not the case. The majority of mothers said that their children followed them around. Therefore, while one might expect the kitchen to be a prohibited area, it was rarely stated as such, because the child was usually near the parent, and the latter was able to 'keep an eye on him'. When asked if the child had a 'favourite' room two-thirds of parents said 'no' and frequently added 'wherever I am'. Where they did state a preference the downstairs rooms of lounge, dining room or kitchen were most often mentioned; these rooms would also be those most frequented by mothers during the day. The lounge or dining room often contained a small corner for the child's toys. So, in comparison to nursery classes and schools and playgroups, children did not have 'free run' of the home; a large minority of children could not enter some rooms and most stayed near their parents. The home environment may be more personal, but it is not necessarily less constrained than nurseries.

We turn now to a more detailed discussion of the child's activities in the context of his home life.

2. Children's experiences prior to entry

With mothers

The majority of our mothers were at home during their children's waking day and said that their children were in their company for most of the day. To distinguish, in some measure, between the mother's physical proximity to, and active involvement with, the child, we asked whether the parent found time during the day to play with her child. 'Play' in this context included all activities where the parent was paying particular attention to the child, either by joining in with toy play, suggesting activities, or making efforts to include the child in the parent's own activities. The answers to this varied considerably. Six per cent said they did not play with their children and a further 41 per cent played for less than an hour a day. Mothers who worked found it more difficult to find time to play with their children but often seemed to be making particular efforts to set aside a special time to sit with them even if it was just to watch television after coming home from work. Another general impression, gathered from those who played for only short periods with their children, was that where the child was the second, third or fourth born, the parents spent less time actually playing or reading stories than they did with their first born. In such cases parents commented that the young child played more with his siblings, or that the brother or sister 'looked after' the youngster and 'kept him amused'. A few parents, no matter how blandly we tried to ask this question, admitted to feelings of guilt on this matter and felt they ought to be playing with their child more often. A few admitted frankly that children's toys did not interest them and that on the whole they found their young children boring to be with and were looking forward to them getting older and becoming more independent. Parents with more than one child seemed to find second and subsequent children 'easier to cope with', 'more contented' and 'less trouble' than the first born. For this reason they said they found it possible to leave the child to his own devices more than they did their first born. This attitude in part may be a function of the mother's more relaxed attitude toward parenthood once the first hurdle had been passed, and the fact that with more than one child her work load is greater and she has less free time available.

Over half the mothers said they found time to play for more than an hour with their children. A few mothers said they spent 'all day' playing with their children but this was unusual and occurred where the mothers appeared exceptionally child-oriented and consciously organized their day to fit around their child's needs and desires. For example one such parent stopped to read to her child whenever he brought her a book and, similarly, joined in his Lego building, puzzle making or other toy play whenever he looked as though he would like her company. Although he was allowed to play unsupervised in the garden, she thought it was 'unstimulating' to leave a child to play on his own and so left him in his own company for only short periods, before joining in or suggesting another activity. This parent also watched children's television with her son since she wished to talk about this or answer his questions on the programmes 'and you can't do that if you haven't seen it'.

More typical were the mothers who said they spent a certain time on household chores – usually mornings – and then spent up to two hours after lunch playing with their children, or after going shopping and before tea and bedtime. Popular activities were reading stories, drawing pictures and looking at books. Over half the mothers said that their children 'helped' them during the chores by having a brush or duster and following them around. Many children enjoyed helping to wash the dishes though as the mothers pointed out this was usually in order to play with the soap bubbles and water. The children also liked helping with pastry making and mothers often gave them a piece of dough to roll and shape. Mothers rarely organized more messy activities requiring supervision, for example, modelling with plasticine or painting. A number said they did not allow this because they worried that the plasticine would get into the carpet or that the child would eat it, or he might spill or drink the paint. Two mothers of young children in one street were unusual in that they had got together to organize and supervise a painting session every week where the other child was invited to share the facilities and experience.

Another activity with mother was listening to stories. Over half the mothers (forty-five) said they read to their children three or more times a week; twenty-six said they read once or twice a week while fifteen said they did not read to their children. In addition, over half the children were read to by someone other than mother; this was usually the father though grand-mothers also read occasionally. Only a small number of children had books from libraries – mothers were worried that they might be torn or scribbled on – but all had story or picture books of their own (63 per cent) or which they shared with their brothers or sisters (37 per cent). The children's own interest in books varied however and 63 per cent were said to like looking at books 'very much', 20 per cent 'to some extent', while eight per cent were said not to like looking at books.

With fathers

Of the fathers in the sample a fifth did not see their children regularly during the working week. This was usually because of shift work or being away on business for a major portion of the week. The majority of fathers however saw their children for up to six hours a day including early morning, breakfast times, lunchtimes if they worked locally, and after work. A small proportion (5 per cent) were accessible to the children for a major part of the day and this occurred when father was unemployed or worked a permanent night shift or, as in two cases, worked for themselves using the home as a base. With regard to playing with their children, 14 per cent of fathers did not find time to play with them, 47 per cent played less than an hour a day with their children, while 39 per cent played for more than an hour each day. Fathers' activities with children were somewhat different to the mothers'. Half of the fathers read, or played games such as snakes and ladders or dominoes (though not as frequently as mothers), and nearly two-thirds played 'rough and tumble' games with their children – the latter activities not being popular with mothers. Fewer fathers than mothers joined in other types of indoor games such as playing with children's toys and fewer involved their children in 'helping' with their activities. Even so, a quarter of fathers involved their children – particularly sons – in activities such as tinkering with the car, gardening and decorating.

Children were also looked after by their fathers several times a week (60 per cent) or occasionally (30 per cent) while a few were never left on their own with father. Fathers tended to have care of the children when the mothers went shopping at weekends or worked evenings. In the latter case a number of fathers provided the children's evening tea, saw to bathing or otherwise got their children ready for bed. The ten per cent of fathers who did not involve themselves tended to work long or awkward hours and their wives had become accustomed to doing everything for the children. One father in this category was exceptional in that although he spent a good deal of time at home he had very little contact with his three girls:

> I don't play much with them. I might read a book but that's very rarely, or very occasionally take them to the shop to fetch a newspaper. When my wife goes to church at weekends I sit with them – though it's usually time for bed. Once the child has got over the shock of it being me instead of her mother she usually settles down.

This father was one of the 21 per cent who were judged to take an insignificant part in their children's lives relative to the time they had available. Forty-two per cent of fathers were considered to take a big part in their children's lives in so far as they spent much of the time they had at home involving themselves with their children or taking them out with them rather than leaving them behind, and 35 per cent took a smaller part than their wives but were still seen as influential figures in their children's lives. A number of mothers, whose husbands worked a 'normal' day, said that they tended to 'hand over' responsibility for the children to them when they come home from work while they themselves got on with preparing the evening meal. However, apart from the fairly common occurrences of fathers making cups of tea, and less often breakfast or supper, there was little evidence of parents sharing the responsibility of their children equally. The traditional pattern of mother as 'housewife' and father as 'worker' still predominated, with the present day difference that mothers might also work outside the home while fathers might help a little more in the house. An isolated case of role sharing in a more complete sense was found in a family where there were four children. Father was a milkman and mother did not work outside the home. The mother described their household as 'a joint one' where she would regularly take over 'father's jobs' such as his daily and weekly accounts while he would take over the cooking, cleaning and playing with the children. Since he was up early and at home by 12.30 p.m. he was able to spend much time with his wife and children; they frequently went out as a family, he also took the younger children with him when he went out and would also take and fetch the older children from school as a matter of course and not merely in 'special' circumstances.

With others

The child's major social contacts with adults were, as expected, with parents. A small proportion of children spent their day with childminders or grand-mothers or with staff of day nurseries. Mothers on the whole were fairly uncertain of the actual time these caretakers spent with the child in one-to-one contacts. Over a third of the children saw other people in their homes frequently, that is, nearly every day. For the main part such visitors were relations and the parents' friends. Just under a third had contact with visitors occasionally, that is, once or twice a week, while a similar proportion rarely saw visitors in their homes. Quite a number of children therefore were unused to regular contact with adults other than parents in their own homes.

Children's contacts with other children also varied considerably. Where they had older brothers and sisters the parents tended to leave the children to play together. Approximately 20 per cent were 'only' children and this situation did not apply. Of those who had siblings, all spent some time during the day with them and for the majority this was up to three or four hours a day. Older siblings tended to play games with the younger and were said to be 'taking more of an interest' as their brother or sister matured. Where the sample child was the oldest the mothers generally attempted to involve him in looking after the baby – letting him 'help' during bath times for example.

The young child's contacts outside the home, with children other than siblings, also varied. Nearly half were said to have frequent contact (three or more times a week) with others of a similar age while 17 per cent had regular, once or twice weekly contact. Over a third however had fairly infrequent contact or none at all. This group tended to include those who were 'only' children and those whose parents had few contacts with other young families. Children of this age are extremely dependent on their parents as a means of bringing them into contact with other children and we take up this question again in a later section since, although the majority of mothers appeared satisfied with their own life outside the home, nearly 40 per cent thought their children needed more opportunities to play with other children and this was given as a main reason for wanting to send children to a pre-school setting. When playing with other children 40 per cent were said to get on 'very well', 48 per cent 'mainly well' with some quarrels, usually over toys, while 12 per cent of the children were described by their parents as 'shy, aggressive or not interested'.

Excursions

Apart from the above contact with children, which usually took place in their own or friends' homes on a sharing of visits basis, most of the children in the sample had been taken out by their parents in the month prior to the interview. Shops were the most frequently visited places; 77 per cent of the children had gone shopping on six or more occasions in the month. Shops were sometimes seen as a source of social contact. One little girl often visited the shop next door by herself in order to talk to the assistants or buy a small item for her mother. The mother allowed her to do this because she felt they would both be isolated for much of the week if it was not for the shop since there was no bus stop near any parks or places of interest within a reasonable distance. Mothers generally found it hard work taking young children shopping but a number used the trips in interesting ways. For example, one mother said they counted the lamp posts or whatever they could see on the way, another that she pointed out the colours of cars. In the shop itself mothers usually allowed their children to put goods into the basket and rather less often provided them with a little money to choose a sweet and pay for it on their own.

Homes of friends and relations were the second most frequented places: 55 per cent of children had been on such visits six or more times during the previous month. There were regular visits to relations living within travelling distance and these often involved the whole family on a Saturday or Sunday. Going for a walk or visiting a park or playgroup were comparatively infrequent activities and the majority of children had made few visits to doctors' or dentists' surgeries, clinics or hospitals for either themselves or other members of their family.

Two-thirds of the children were said to have gone out every day during the week prior to the interviews but these outings were often of short duration and the majority of the children spent the major part of their waking day in their homes and gardens with mother as their main companion.

Activities

Table 3.2 gives some idea of the kinds of play materials mothers said their children spent their time with in the home.

Table 3.2: The frequency with which children contacted play materials at home.

Activity/Toy Type	Percentage of children		
	Often	Occasionally	Rarely
1. Pencil or crayons and paper	86	12	2
2. Bicycles, tricycles, scooters, etc.	74	23	4
3. Cars, trains, etc.	65	20	15
4. Dolls, soft toys	63	13	24
5. Building and construction toys	55	30	15
6. Push, pull type toys	37	24	38
7. Toys for music making	34	37	30
8. Puzzles and jigsaws	31	33	36
9. Dressing-up outfits	19	35	47
10. Paint	19	44	37
11. Plasticine, clay, etc.	12	33	56

Note: Percentages have been rounded up or down and rows may not, therefore, total 100 per cent.

The relationship between these activities and the sex of the children was examined and the analysis indicated that there were statistically significant differences between the girls and boys in the kind of activities they did at home. More boys than girls played frequently with construction toys, such as bricks and Lego.[1] Boys also played more often with small cars, trucks, trains or aeroplanes. The girls played far more frequently than boys with soft toys or dolls and push pull types of toy (in which prams and brick trolleys were included). To some extent these differences reflect the opportunities which children had to encounter toy materials. In all-girl or boy households the child was less likely to have toys bought for them which are regarded as appropriate to the other sex. For example, in a few all-girl households there was a noticeable lack of toy cars, trains, aeroplanes and construction toys and a converse emphasis on dolls and soft toys. While boys sometimes played with 'action men' dolls, they less frequently had access to the usual 'girls'' dolls especially where there were no girls in the family. However, such single sex situations did not apply to the majority of children and, although a small minority of them had very little in the way of toys, most had a good variety of playthings. Many girls did have bricks and toy cars to play with and both sexes frequently had Fisher Price or similar toys which require fitting pieces together and are intended to stimulate learning and imaginative play. On the whole girls appeared to have rather more variety of toys than boys since they often had traditionally boys' toys as well as girls': it seems it is more acceptable to buy toy cars for a girl than it would be to buy a doll for a boy. One mother commented that she thought her children had far too much in the way of toys. Her younger child had access to his sister's toys as well as a room full of his own. This mother felt that as a result he never seemed to 'settle to anything for long', that he had 'little concentration' and hardly ever completed a task 'such as a puzzle or a simple game'. In two households, where the families were clearly living in circumstances below the poverty line, the children seemed to spend much of their time sitting around doing nothing, interspersed with periods of 'fighting' when they would poke each other and roll around until told to behave. Such toys as they had – a broken toy car in one case and lopsided tricycle and a ball with a bell inside in another – were well-used and past their prime.

A likely source of differences in play behaviour are differences in the ways that boys and girls are treated from the moment of birth. These are likely to have an accumulative effect which results in strong differences in the way children behave by the time they are three-years-old. That mother and father behave differently towards their child was indicated earlier and even where they believe they treat their boys and girls alike, their own different behaviour patterns must remain as a contradictory reality for the child himself. One mother for example described her little girl as 'rather more like a boy, a tomboy really'. This parent insisted she was prepared to tolerate this beha-

[1] In order not to interrupt the text all statistical results are presented in Appendix 1.

viour but clearly believed it to be deviant, as 'not normal for a girl' and as a behaviour pattern which needed to be justified by reference to 'equality of the sexes'. When asked about 'dressing up' activities some mothers interpreted this to mean whether or not the children took an interest in the clothes they wore and it had to be explained that by this we meant pretend play involving taking on another character; this occurred far more where the young child was a girl than a boy.

Television

Another regular daily activity for most of the children was watching television. All the homes except one had a television set, a quarter of these being black and white and the rest coloured. In a small minority of homes the television set was left on for the major part of the child's waking day and provided general background noise but in only two cases was the set left on while the interview took place. Parents were asked firstly to say how long the set was on during the day and secondly how long the child actually sat and watched it. Over a third of the televisions were on for more than four hours during the child's waking hours; six per cent were on for less than an hour; 17 per cent for up to two hours; 17 per cent for up to three hours and 20 per cent for up to four hours. The majority of children (60 per cent) actually watched television for half an hour to up to two hours a day; a further 17 per cent watched it for two to three hours a day while 12 per cent watched for less than half an hour a day. A small number of children (seven per cent), described as television fanatics by their parents, watched for more than three hours a day or for as long as the television was available. The children appeared to differ considerably in terms of how long they would sit and concentrate on a programme. A few parents said that their children were unable to sit still for more than a minute at a time but others that they would sit as if mesmerized for hours.

Parents tended not to censor television viewing for their children (74 per cent). The main reason given for this attitude was that the programmes on during the day were relatively harmless and the children tended to watch only the children's programmes anyway. Some parents believed that 'at this age' children only take in certain aspects of what they see and thought that they would filter out any violence that arose while they were watching (in this respect the news programmes were seen as most likely to present unacceptable images), or simply not understand sexual references where they arose in adult programmes during the day. The rest of the parents (26 per cent) tended to turn off the television or ensure it was not put on when certain programmes were due and, while parents mentioned scenes involving violence, use of firearms and sexual crudity, they were unable to name any particular programmes, since they felt these were matters which could arise

unexpectedly, for example in the news, afternoon films or discussion programmes.

In general, parents approved of television for its entertainment value and
for its potential as a learning medium in teaching children songs, rhymes,
colour or counting. Sometimes they expressed surprise at their children's
learning. For instance one child enjoyed watching the schools' programmes
and learned to sing a song in French. One father, a recent immigrant with
his family, particularly emphasized the value of television as a means of helping his children learn about British culture and traditions. Most mothers said
they watched television with their children, but this was usually for less time
than their children watched. Many parents used this time while their children were occupied to get on with food preparation or for jobs where the child
might be in the way, for instance, one mother said she would tackle 'dirty or
messy jobs like cleaning the toilet' and another that she might wash her hair.
A minority of parents ensured that they watched particular programmes,
usually those they considered to have an educational content, in order to
answer the child's questions or be able to carry out suggested activities.

By way of concluding this discussion of physical and social characteristics
of the home environment, we can now identify several specific differences
between home and the pre-school. The child's usual physical environment
will be less spacious, typically restricted to the same room his mother is in,
with brief visits outside, particularly to the shops. Though some mothers
put aside a certain length of time to interact on a relatively exclusive basis
with their children, the social interaction with parents is generally not as
intense as might be expected; mothers may be in the same place but doing
something else while fathers are around far less frequently and actually
interact, in a playful fashion, relatively infrequently. Nevertheless, interaction will occur on a one-to-one basis more frequently than could be
expected in pre-school where there are likely to be more children relative to
adults. Much social interaction takes place with siblings, and only children
therefore experience a very different social environment in comparison to
those children with brothers and sisters. There was strong evidence of
different activities being provided for boys and girls. One implication of this
concerns the different expectations the sexes will have acquired very early in
life, and which they will bring to the nursery. Without direction from pre-
school staff, it seems likely that this sex-typical behaviour will continue in
the pre-school. Pre-school staff may have a special role in not allowing this
process to consolidate into entrenched behaviour patterns during the early
and sensitive years.

3. Parental attitudes to learning

The interview contained questions designed to provide insight into, firstly, the kind of things which parents saw as being important for their child to learn about and, secondly, their attitudes towards the type of learning which might be assumed to be fostered within pre-school provision for the younger child.

Seventy-two per cent of parents felt there were things it was important their child learn at home. Learning of a 'social' nature was mentioned by 54 per cent of these parents. In this category were placed responses such as 'learning to share', 'to play with others' and 'learning to say please and thank you'. Manners in general were mentioned frequently whilst moral instruction – such as learning 'that other people matter', 'learning right from wrong' – was specified somewhat less often. Sometimes the learning of good conduct towards animals was stated as valuable training for the child in acquiring kindness and patience. 'Educational' learning was mentioned by 40 per cent of the group and responses relating to the learning of colours, numbers, stories, rhymes and so on came into this category. Learning about safety was mentioned as important by 25 per cent of the group. Parents here emphasized the importance of learning to play safely inside and outside the home. They said their children were 'into everything', mentioning the child's fascination with electrical sockets, matches, fires, irons, kettles and cookers and they therefore attempted to form a barrier between their children and potentially dangerous situations, while trying to teach them there were certain things they simply must not so.

The remainder of the parents (28 per cent), who did not think there was anything of particular importance for the child to learn, offered two different reasons for this opinion: either that 'everything' was important at this age, or, that 'at this age they (children) can't do much can they?' Parents responding in the latter way seemed to assume that the kind of learning we wished to know about was of a formal nature such as that they expected to find in schools. Learning such as this they saw as involving specific teaching of educational subjects and they did not think this kind of learning could take place prior to school entry.

From the ways in which parents answered our questions on learning it seems clear that they not only differentiated between types of learning but also between what they considered were important things for their children to learn about. As we have said, parents tended to give priority to learning of a social nature, with educational learning given a lower priority. Despite this, many parents said, in answer to more direct questions on learning, that they tried to encourage such learning. Most parents encouraged their children to learn numbers, patterned speech (such as nursery rhymes), and colours, in that order. Three-quarters said they helped to point out shapes of things to their children while just over half said they were helping children learn the alphabet. Less help was given over teaching to tell the time (37 per cent) and very little in teaching to read (nine per cent). Over half the parents however said that they would definitely try to help their children to read before going to school (at five-years-old) and a greater proportion (71 per cent) that they would definitely help with writing. On the matter of reading, a further fifth of the parents said they would help if their child showed interest and 13 per cent would help if they knew how to do so. With regard to writing, a further fifth of the parents said they would help if their children showed interest and four per cent if they knew how to help. These findings indicate that parents were more reluctant to help with reading than they were with writing. They appeared to lack confidence in attempting to teach their children to read and of the small number who were already trying to help most had had a reasonable education themselves, or had trained as teachers or had helped in playgroups. This experience appeared to have given them a greater under-standing of the importance of the steps leading up to actual reading of the printed word and they appeared to be utilizing their children's initiatives in associating pictures with words in books, as for example on cereal packets and tinned goods. Many other parents may have been helping their children's pre-reading skills, for example while reading to them and looking at books, but seemed unaware that they were doing so and did not think of this or other everyday actions as helping their children learn to read.

When asked whether they, as parents, can have an effect on their children's development, 69 per cent believed they could have a marked effect, but responses frequently referred to setting examples of good behaviour in the social or moral sense and not to mental or educational development. Other parents (27 per cent) felt that parents could effect a child's development to some extent but that his own nature would prevent the parent having a marked effect; five per cent believed that parents had little effect on the way their child developed.

These indications of parent attitude towards their children's development may help those involved in educational activities – particularly at pre-school level – decide on the best courses of action to involve parents in the school life of their children. Parents, as we have seen, tended to give priority to social learning over educational learning for their children aged between two-and-a-half and three-and-a-half-years-old. This emphasis seems to stem partly from the parents' natural concern for the physical and emotional well-being of their children and partly from their general lack of understand-ing regarding the potential capacity that their children also have for develop-ment in the cognitive sense – for learning of the type which parents tend to see as taking place in schools. Parents tend to undervalue their own influence and potential as vital factors in their children's learning except over matters where they see themselves as competent. Those concerned to involve parents fully in the child's early years outside the home environment should therefore make every effort to help parents understand how and why they do certain things at pre-school since this will tend to demystify the education scene for the parents and hopefully give them more confidence to pursue related activities at home and thereby reinforce learning at pre-school. Since many parents believe they can and do influence their child's development, a reasonable degree of cooperation might be available provided they understand what is required of them. This cooperation will however probably be more forthcoming on an individual basis because parents tend to have a different general outlook from that of staff. At the risk of stating the obvious, parents are concerned for their own children while staff divide their interest among many. The personal approach to parents as individuals would therefore seem to be the most fruitful way of pursuing involvement if, that is, staff wish to enlist parent cooperation. Many parents were trying to help their children and it would be a pity if the most were not made of this after the child enters pre-school.

4. Pre-school provision: parents' knowledge and choice of setting

Knowledge

Parents were asked a number of questions about pre-school provisions in general and in their locality in particular. At a general level the majority were able to name the major forms of pre-school provision. Playgroups were usually mentioned first followed by nurseries then, with less frequency, childminders, creches and day-care nurseries. Mother and baby clubs were mentioned infrequently, and few mothers had ever gone to one. Reference to playgroup as 'playschool' frequently occurred and is possibly due to the widespread popularity of the television programme of the same name. A few parents discussed the possible disparity of provision in different regions of the country. On the whole though parents had difficulty in separating the knowledge they had of the local situation from that which might pertain at a national level. Since the former often reflected the state of provision in general, the distinction seems of little practical significance.

One point which deserves particular emphasis is that parents mentioned 'childminders' or 'day-care nurseries' far less frequently than playgroups and nurseries, while specific questions on local day-care provision were frequently met with what might be called a 'stone-wall' response. Not only were nearly two-thirds of the parents ignorant of any such local provision but a number simply refused to consider them. Some mothers for instance, replied to the question asking 'where would you go to find out more about day care?' with variations of the following: 'I don't know and to be frank, I wouldn't want to know'. Day-care services are quickly taken up when offered, indicating the need for such services, but there was little demand for them among the interviewed mothers. Their marked lack of enthusiasm was being sustained on two fronts it seemed. Firstly, there was an 'ideology' of motherhood which enabled mothers looking after their children at home to feel justified in doing so and sometimes adopt a superior attitude towards those who did not. Despite small steps towards equality between the sexes, the prevailing ethos among these mothers was that it was not 'right' to go out to work if that necessitated someone else looking after your child. The second reason for lack of enthusiasm was negative feelings towards day care services as such. State day nurseries were regarded as inadequate substitutes which could not meet standards of care found in the home; moreover mothers did not want to be numbered among those either forced to work or unable to cope at home.

The exceptions to this unenthusiastic attitude towards day care were found among single parents who needed day care services and the few parents who had had prior personal contacts with day nurseries. Among the latter were two mothers who became ill and their children were taken into a day nursery until they became better. For the six per cent of single parent families the local provisions did not seem to meet their needs. Two mothers had children in a day nursery and now that their children were three-years-old they wanted to move them into an ordinary nursery class. They felt that in the day nursery the emphasis was on care and health and that this was not sufficiently stimulating for the older toddler. They believed that their children should mix with 'ordinary' children and perhaps make some friends before going into infant school. These parents realized however that the nursery class or school usually offered a half-day place, and even if the staff could be persuaded to offer a full-time place the day would still be too short for them to continue working. One mother was offered a full-time place in a nursery class and arranged for her friends to collect her son and take him to school. The other, who had been prepared to try and adjust her working hours, was not offered a full-time place and her son had to continue in day care until the time came for full-time school. Another mother lived at home with her parents, brothers and sisters in a three-generation household. She was unhappy with the fact that her child spent most of the day with a childminder while she worked. This mother would have preferred him to spend at least a morning at playgroup or nursery now that he was two-and-a-half-years-old. This was not possible due to the age restrictions rapidly being introduced by playgroups in her area and already existing for nursery classes and schools. Her dissatisfaction with the situation had led to her arranging for her young sister to take her child to the childminder on the way to school and collect him on her way home thereby reducing the hours he spent with the childminder. The remaining single parents staying at home found it difficult to make ends meet. One of these mothers relied a great deal on support from her parents, could not afford to buy a newspaper regularly and felt isolated from other families nearby.

We found that a few parents had very little knowledge of the more prevalent forms of pre-school provision – playgroups and nurseries – either nationally or locally. They had in common a relatively low level of contact with other mothers of children under five. Such isolation arose for a number of reasons. For example, one mother was much older than the average age for mothers of two-and-a-half-year-olds. Her young daughter was almost a generation removed from her siblings; one brother being 17-years-old and the other 19. This parent admitted to knowing 'hardly anything' of provisions. None of her contemporaries or friends had children as young as her daughter who, therefore, had little scope for contact with other young children except in shops where she would 'stare at them and look a bit wary'. The health visitor had told this parent about a local playgroup, but the mother was unsure of the age at which her child could be sent or what the playgroup did. This mother's age had tended to isolate her from the younger mothers' grapevine and the extent of her knowledge was the same as when she had her first two children: 'My sons never went to playgroup, there wasn't anything like that then'.

Younger mothers could also be isolated from their contemporaries. Moving home seemed to be a contributing factor. A move to a new area could break contacts with mothers they may have met while attending clinics or hospital during pregnancy and childbirth, and could also break other neighbourhood friendships. One young mother who had recently moved into a council flat gave an additional explanation for her lack of friends or associates. She felt that her teenage pregnancy and very early marriage had cut her off from school friends. She also said that other tenants in nearby flats appeared to be very much older than herself and her husband. These tenants were rarely seen during the week, being out at work for the most part. The regular contacts for this mother and child were restricted to visiting her own mother a few times a week, her husband's mother once a week and her cousin perhaps every six to eight weeks.

These cases of social isolation fortunately appeared to be rare. They serve to emphasize the point that the majority of parents interviewed relied heavily on 'neighbours', 'friends' and 'relations' for their information about the local pre-school scene. Table 3.3 lists how mothers obtained their information

Table 3.3: Source of parents' information on pre-school provisions.

Sources of information	Nursery	Playgroup	Day-care
	%	%	%
Neighbours, friends	47	48	14
Relations	17	5	2
Advertisements in shops, newspapers	2	8	2
Advertisements in, or visits to, clinics, doctors, library, official depts.	14	23	16
Proximity to provision and others	11	8	9
No source i.e. parent unaware of provision nearby	9	8	57
Total	100(n = 86)	100(n = 86)	100(n = 86)

about provision. Information about nurseries and playgroups was predominantly obtained through word of mouth, though playgroups appeared to have a broader system of advertising than nurseries. Information about day care again differed in that it came mainly through visits to, or advertisements seen at, clinics, doctors, libraries. Over half the parents did not know whether there was any such provision. Regarding clinics we can add that mothers said they did not attend all that frequently now their children were two-and-a-half-years-old. Our findings indicate that no particular place springs to parents' minds when they are asked where would they go to find out more about provision. One parent said that there appeared to be 'no obvious place to go'. Parents mentioned that they might try the clinic, library, health visitor, Citizens' Advice Bureau and the local authority education or health departments.

Leaving aside the question of the accuracy of parents' knowledge, we can say that the majority had favourable attitudes towards playgroups and nurseries and had decided to send their children to one or the other when they were old enough. The exceptions were interesting in that they indicated that they felt under some pressure to follow the trend and send their child to a pre-school setting such as a playgroup. For example one mother had a son of twelve by a previous marriage and a young son. She had brought up the oldest child alone and felt that by having to work to support him she had missed his early years of growing up. She did not feel that there was much affection or contact between them. This mother seemed determined that this should not be repeated for herself and her younger boy. She frankly admitted to being 'a possessive mother', not liking to let the child out of her sight or being separated in any way. She thought, however, that this attitude of hers might be detrimental to her son and although she did not really want to send him to playgroup, she thought that she might do so 'for his sake' so that he could make friends with children.

Another mother had two children under five. The older boy was to start school soon and he had not attended a playschool or nursery. She was friendly with a few mothers having similarly aged children and occasionally had children in to play with her own. She felt that the individual attention she gave to teaching her children was likely to stimulate their development better than the divided attention they would receive at playgroup or nursery. Her friends, she said, 'think I am mad to keep them at home'. She was having second thoughts about her decision now that her son was nearing school age. She thought that this would leave her young daughter without anyone to play with since the children who came to the house were nearer to her son's age and would also be starting school. This mother was the only one to explicitly mention a dual role with regard to her children: 'I feel more like a teacher sometimes as well as being a mother ... I do make them sit down and read or draw or do other things'. This parent had no teaching experience but had looked after other people's children in her former occupation as a nanny. She felt that she provided a disciplined routine in the home which would enable her children to fit easily into a school situation. She held a more favourable attitude towards nurseries since she thought they were better disciplined with teacher-trained staff and that they would teach the children rather than let them 'play all the time' as she believed playgroups did.

With regard to the age of entry to nurseries and playgroups, thirty-six per cent of parents were not sure of the minimum age in the case of nurseries, whilst thirty per cent were unclear in the case of playgroups. Confusion had arisen over the age of playgroup entry since many mothers believed there had been recent changes in their area. Most were fairly certain that the age was now three years while thirty per cent thought it might still be two-and-a-half but were uncertain. Ten per cent did not know at all. Mothers gave confused explanations as to why this change had occurred. A few thought there must have been a change in 'the law'. Others thought that the change in local authority 'regulations' meant that if playgroups accepted children under three years, they had to take on extra helpers and most playgroups could not afford to do this. During the course of this survey we came across a firm body of opinion among mothers that raising the age of playgroup entry to three was not acceptable to them as potential users of playgroups. Such an opinion was consistent with their beliefs that young children were 'ready to contact' other children from birth (73 per cent) or at least by the time they were two-years-old (a further 15 per cent of parents). The majority of parents believed that by the time a child was two-and-a-half he or she needed regular contact with other children. This will be elaborated in the next section as one of the major reasons parents gave for desiring pre-school provisions.

To conclude this section on parents' knowledge of existing provisions in their area, we would add that despite the growth of 'mother and toddler clubs' there was a severe lack of awareness or knowledge about them among the mothers. Only a small minority of mothers interviewed had attended such a club. Of these, only two continued to attend for at least a year for the purposes of finding friends with children the same age as their own. One mother said it had taken 'great persistence' on her part to keep attending and felt that many mothers would have given up trying but she had been determined to build up a circle of women with children whom she knew well enough to invite home. As soon as this objective was achieved she gave up the club, finding it far more satisfactory to have a few mothers and children visit her home, and she their homes, because this provided a quieter atmosphere for the children and was friendlier for the parents. Those parents who had attended mother and toddler clubs once or twice, said that they were 'too noisy', 'undisciplined', 'more for the mothers than the children' and had found them unsatisfactory. The poor image of mother and toddler clubs persisted even among mothers who had never attended one. They felt it was not for them; it was just not their scene to 'gossip with other mothers, whilst surrounded by noisy children'.

Choice of setting and reasons for choosing pre-school experience

Eighty-three of the 86 parents wanted to send their children to some form of pre-school provision. The parents who had expressed definite interest in sending their children to pre-school were asked to say which setting they would choose. Table 3.4 sets out the responses of these interested parents.

Table 3.4: Parents' choice of setting.

Setting	Percentage of parents choosing setting
Nursery class	49
Nursery school	10
Playgroup then nursery class or school	15
Playgroup	23
Day care	0
Childminder	1
Other (e.g. private kindergarten)	2
Total	100 (n = 83)

Given freedom of choice nearly 60 per cent of parents would have liked a nursery setting while a further fifteen per cent would have liked playgroup followed by nursery attendance for their children. Twenty-three per cent of parents said they would choose a playgroup. Five out of the six mothers with children at a childminder would choose alternative settings if these were adapted to suit their needs. Similarly, none of the parents wanted their children to be in day care; even those few who already had a child attending state day nurseries opted for an alternative.

On the matter of choice of provision parents are clearly constrained by what is available and even though the majority of parents would have liked nursery education for their children they believed this was not a realistic option. Our sample is probably generously weighted towards those who could actually send their child to a nursery class or school since nearly a third of those interviewed were drawn from registers of nursery classes for the purpose of later observation. This poses difficulties in attempting to assess how satisfied parents appeared to be with the choice of provision for the under-fives. Certainly many mothers, when asked about such provisions, said bluntly that in their opinion there was not enough available. Those who did not have a nursery class or school in their immediate area expressed general dissatisfaction with the level of provision. Where they were available mothers mentioned long waiting lists for a place and as one mother put it, 'You practically have to put their names down when they are born to stand a chance'. In view of the limited amount of nursery provision, not all parents have freedom of choice except perhaps between playgroups.

A significant factor influencing parents' ultimate choice of setting was therefore availability. They would tend to be influenced by what was practical and, faced with the uncertainty of obtaining a place at nursery at some unspecified time in the future, many mothers knew that they would choose the certainty of playgroup as the first, and very probably only, setting for their three-year-olds.

The mothers' comments suggested other factors which might influence choice. For example, parents with children at playgroup highlighted the advantages, as they saw them, of playgroups over nurseries. Firstly there was usually a playgroup in close proximity to their home, a vital factor for mothers without their own transport (only 29 per cent of the sample had the regular use of a car). Secondly, they were able to send their children to a morning session and most mothers wanted this. Thirdly, parents felt they could choose the number of sessions a child attended each week, whereas a nursery expected attendance on every day. One mother explained that attendance every day would not be satisfactory for her: 'I like to whizz about and don't want to be tied every day to picking him up and taking him to nursery. I would miss him anyway. I enjoy his company and take him out with me a lot. We can go shopping all day and will have lunch out, he likes that.'

Playgroups were seen therefore, by some parents, as convenient in terms of proximity to their homes and in allowing choice over frequency and time of attendance. Against this they mentioned the disadvantage of their cost. One mother thought that this would deter poorer parents from sending their children to playgroup and two mothers in very difficult economic circumstances said that they felt 60 pence a morning was 'rather a lot of money to find'. Paradoxically, the fact that nurseries are free was mentioned as a possible disadvantage by a few mothers. For example one said that she would choose a state nursery class if a place were available but would be worried by it having more children from socially disadvantaged homes because it was free. Whilst careful not to appear snobbish, she did not like to think that her child might come home using swear words or using poorer language in a grammatical sense.

A further factor which could affect the parents' choice of pre-school setting, whether nursery or playgroup, is their familiarity with the setting. If their other children or friends' or relatives' children have attended a particular place parents had more confidence in making their decision. They feel they 'know' that the facilities are reasonable and would be satisfactory for their children and they would tend not to explore other pre-school provisions which might be available. As we mentioned earlier, parents relied heavily on friends, neighbours and other mothers for information regarding pre-school provision and it seems that word-of-mouth 'recommendation', in the absence of first-hand knowledge, carried a great deal of weight when parents decide on a particular form of provision for their children.

Table 3.5 summarizes other aspects of the provision parents would like for their children at nursery and playgroup.

Table 3.5: Summary of provision required by parents in ideal choice situation.

	Nursery n = 77	Playgroup n = 50
	%	%
Desired age at start – 2–3 years	49	86
– 3–4 years	45	12
– 4–5 years	5	2
Number of sessions a week at start – 1	4	4
– 2	21	70
– 3	13	6
– 4	0	2
– 5	65	18
Full-time attendance	8	2
Part-time attendance – am	71	88
– pm	21	10

Note: Percentages may not equal 100 due to rounding.

Seventy-seven parents answered the questions regarding desired nursery schools or class provisions, while fifty mothers, who had not already been offered a nursery place, also answered the questions regarding playgroups. The table to a great extent reflects parents' understanding of each situation, that is, that nurseries do not often take children under three whereas play-groups used to – and still ought to in their view. One of the most interesting findings was that 38 per cent of parents would have liked their children to build up slowly to the everyday attendance usually required by nurseries.

Apart from the factors relating to choice of setting, the interviews attempted to elicit parents' reasons for wanting their children to attend pre-school in the first place. These were obtained in two ways from those parents expressing interest in pre-school. Firstly, they were asked to state their main reasons for wanting this experience for their children. In discussing these results information drawn from parents' descriptions of nurseries and playgroups is used and the distinctions and similarities parents believed existed between the two types of provision will become clearer.

Table 3.6 indicates that over half the parents put forward social aspects as a reason for desiring pre-school provision for their child. Parents stated their belief that their children should have the companionship of other children. They wanted them to learn to mix, learn to share, and learn how to play with other children. As was stated earlier the majority of parents (64 per cent) believed that children should be with other children from the time they are born and a further 16 per cent thought this was necessary by the age of two. A reason often put forward for this was so that they would become accustomed to the presence of children. Parents suggested that you could not

Table 3.6: Parents' main reasons for wanting child to attend pre-school[1]

Type of reason	Percentage response
Social	55
Educational	28
Personal freedom (for parents)	22
Others	8
Not known (i.e. not asked)	6

[1] More than one reason could be given; column does not therefore total 100 per cent.

expect a child to react very happily when suddenly confronted with a large group of children at around two-and-a-half to three, and even less so at the age of four or five if the child had had only a minimal experience of contact with other children. At this point however parents sometimes distinguished between the situations where a child is merely in the presence of other children and the situations where a child is beginning to 'really play' with another child or a group of children. For the latter situations they suggested that, depending on the individual child's development, this occurred between the ages of 18 months to three years.

Educational reasons for desiring pre-school provision, or those which related to 'preparing' the child for school, were not stressed quite as much overall as the social reasons; in response to the open question 28 per cent of parents gave these as their main reasons. Only two parents spontaneously mentioned the concept of 'learning through play'. This item subsequently received a relatively important rating on the 'reasons grid' (to be shortly discussed) but it was the only item incorporating the word 'learn' in other than a social sense and it is by no means certain that parents were aware of its meaning as used by educationalists. Parents' comments indicated that they did not necessarily associate learning with playing, and that they more often thought of them as separate. For example one mother said of a playgroup: 'I think it's mainly for playing, though we do have a qualified teacher at ours who does seem to try to teach the older children a few things in preparation for school or nursery'. Another mother drew a finer line between play and learning but she was one of the few to do so: 'I hope that in the nursery play is geared towards actual learning rather than play for the sake of play, and would hope that they would start the fundamentals of reading and writing though I would not expect them to actually do reading and writing'. This mother expected directed activities of a pre-reading nature such as pattern recognition games and other activities such as tracing and copying, to help with the acquisition of writing skills. It seemed that most parents saw play as valuable in the pre-school setting as a means whereby children acquire the social skills necessary for cooperative play. This is as much as the majority expected of playgroups but from a nursery they expected more in the way of organized activities directed towards the child's cognitive development.

They also differentiated between playgroups and nurseries when indicating how well these settings would prepare their children for school. They believed that nurseries were more organized, had more of a routine and were more disciplined. One mother said:

> The nursery has a far more planned and structured day. David did some quite good things at playgroup but they did not wring the maximum out of him. Playgroups are more haphazard as far as encouraging intellectual development goes. They could become boring for bright children if they stay there too long.

However, parents seemed to appreciate any pre-school setting for the way in which it gradually introduces the child to a routine, in a place outside their homes, in readiness for the step into full-time schooling.

The second way we assessed parents' reasons for wanting pre-school provision for their child was by asking them to answer the 'reasons grid' which nursery and playgroup staff had completed (the results of which were presented in the last chapter). It will be remembered that respondents were asked to rate 15 reasons for desiring pre-school provision in terms of their importance. Results of these for parents are shown in Table 3.7, where differences to the views of playgroup and nursery staff are also presented. Reference to Table 2.11 (page 48) may be helpful in order to further compare the views of parents and pre-school staff.

The first point of note is the generally lower level of importance that parents attached to most of the reasons. This is seen in the higher mean scores, and the significant differences found by statistical analysis, on most of the items. Overall, then, parents do not attach as much importance to pre-school attendance as do pre-school staff.

Looking at differences in the importance attached to individual items, parents, like playgroup staff, considered 'enabling a child to contact other

Table 3.7: Parents' reasons for desiring pre-school attendance.

	Reason	Mean[1]	rank	Differences between parents' and playgroup and nursery staff's views – were they statistically significant?[2]	
				Playgroup staff	Nursery school/ class staff
1)	Enabling mothers to understand their children	3.32	15	Yes (parents see this reason as less important)	Yes (parents see this reason as less important)
2)	Enabling a child to learn through play	1.48	4	,,	,,
3)	Preparation for later school life	1.42	2		Yes (parents see this as more important)
4)	Enabling a child to contact other adults	2.68	11	,,	Yes (parents see this as less important)
5)	Enabling a child to talk and listen and develop intellectual skills	1.65	5		,,
6)	Enabling a child to develop coordination, balance and other physical skills	2.05	10	,,	,,
7)	Enabling a child to contact other children	1.37	1	,,	
8)	Enabling a child to be more independent	1.89	9	,,	,,
9)	Enabling mothers to have more time to themselves and their own activities	3.18	14		Yes (parents see this reason as more important)
10)	Enabling a child to become part of a group	1.86	8	,,	

Table 3.7—contd.

	Reason	Mean[1]	rank	Differences between parents' and playgroup and nursery staff's views – were they statistically significant?[2]	
				Playgroup staff	Nursery school/class staff
11)	Enabling mothers to meet and get advice from staff	2.76	12		Yes (parents see this reason as less important)
12)	Enabling a child to engage in activities he couldn't easily do at home, e.g., messy play or use of apparatus like climbing frames	1.66	6	,,	
13)	Enabling a child to learn how to share and behave with other children	1.43	3	,,	
14)	Enabling mothers to make friends with other mothers	3.08	13	,,	
15)	Enabling a child to gain a lasting educational advantage	1.85	7		

[1] Scores on each item ranged from 1–5, 1 being the most important, 5 the least important. Therefore the higher the mean score the least important an item on the grid was thought to be.

[2] See Appendix 1 for details of statistical analyses and results.

children' to be the most important reason for pre-school attendance. Interestingly, parents considered the benefits of pre-school attendance as a 'preparation for later school life' to be second in importance. This was one of the few items which parents considered to be more important than did pre-school staff. So although parents recognize the value of pre-school for their child's social development, they are also strongly aware of it as a stepping stone toward school life. Taken in conjunction with the generally lower importance attached to all items this suggests that parents see pre-school not so much as an end in itself, but more in terms of how it can affect later school progress. This is also seen in the lower importance parents attached to most of the items expressing specific benefits to children, i.e. learning through play (item 2), contacting other adults (item 4), development of coordination, balance and other physical skills (item 6) and independence (item 8).

One of the most interesting findings was the tendency for mothers to view the benefits of pre-school attendance to themselves as being of least importance. In this they were in accord with pre-school staff (see Chapter 2). Of lowest importance was 'enabling mothers to understand their children', followed by 'enabling mothers to have more time to themselves' and 'enabling mothers to make friends with other mothers'. What is more, in comparison to pre-school staff, they generally saw benefits to themselves as less important. Only on 'enabling mothers to have more time to themselves' did they attach more importance though this actually owes more to the extremely low importance attached to this by nursery class/school staff.

Overall then, mothers saw less benefit in pre-school attendance in comparison with pre-school staff, with little personal benefit to themselves, and some suggestion that its main benefit was as a useful preparation for school.

5. Entering pre-school: contact desired and anticipated reactions of parent and child

All parents interested in sending their child to pre-school were asked what type of contact they would like with a nursery school or class prior to entry. A large number said they wanted to be able to visit the nursery informally with their child and spend time there (80 per cent). They also wanted to meet individually the staff who would be in charge of their child (65 per cent), while a quarter also wanted an individual chat with the head teacher. Few parents said they would not want any contact beforehand and when they said this it was usually because they had already met the staff and been into the nursery with an older child. Very few parents wanted to visit the nursery or meet the head as part of a group of other mothers. In the last chapter we saw that group visits to the nursery prior to entry accounted for 12 per cent of all visits and in this they are in accord with parents' preferences for individual visits. On the other hand it was our impression that schools had a more formal approach to individual visits than that favoured by parents. A number of parents, for example, wished during a visit, to sit quietly and observe what activities were going on and gain an overall impression of the nursery and staff. Some said they did not want it to be a 'special occasion' but would prefer to become, as one mother put it, 'a fly on the wall' and observe in an unobtrusive way. They wished to see how their child might 'fit in' to the situation and gain some idea of how their child reacted to the other children and the staff and vice versa.

The majority of parents felt that their visit to the nursery would be more important than visits the staff (of a nursery) might wish to make to their home: 'It's more important to take the child to visit the school. It might help parents to talk to them in your own home. But what would be of value is to go along and see how she would fit in with them.'

In the light of the discussion in Chapter 2, on home visits by nursery and playgroup staff, it is interesting to note that 40 per cent of parents said that they would welcome such a visit but would want this in addition to, and not instead of, a visit to the nursery. Parents rarely saw such a visit as helping the staff; they thought the extra work involved might not be worthwhile. Mothers thought such visits would help them and their children get to know the staff in the more relaxed atmosphere of their own home, that the visit would show their children that the teacher was a friend and that such a meeting would help the child settle down at nursery. Some parents also felt they could ask questions of staff on such an occasion. One mother putting this view had little confidence in her own judgment of what was suitable for her son:

> I know very little about children. I've never been around them. I don't really know how they develop or what they are capable of. When the new baby arrived I could see that I had been underestimating Paul's potential and only realized then how quickly he was growing up – he wasn't a baby any more. I would like to find out (of pre-school) *what* they do, *how* they do it and *why*. I spent so many hours watching TV, as a child, that I lost the art of playing. I would want to visit the nursery with Paul to give him confidence before he starts. It will be interesting to see how the other children are.

This clear expression of uncertainty over the upbringing of her children was not typical of our mothers in general. However we gained an impression that parents with one child, or with a first born of only two-and-a-half to three years, sometimes felt inadequate in recognizing whether their children were developing 'normally' or whether they were doing the right thing. Such uncertainty tended to disappear among parents with older children but does suggest that staff in pre-school might make extra efforts to provide guidelines for activities and play materials for mothers with one, or only young children, since they have no older children to use as reference points when comparing and contrasting the development of their youngest children.

Approximately two-thirds of the sample answered questions regarding entry into playgroups. The rest were not asked since they were definitely sending their child to a nursery. Of those responding, 15 per cent said they would not want any prior contact with the playgroup, which is rather higher than those answering for nursery attendance. However, a similar proportion of parents (73 per cent) wanted an informal visit to the playgroup with their children for reasons similar to those given above for nursery. Again on playgroup entry, 56 per cent (contrasted with 65 per cent for the nursery) wanted an individual chat with the playgroup supervisor. Few parents wanted to visit playgroups as part of a group of mothers and children.

All other questions regarding reactions of child and parent on entry, subsequent involvement and contact were asked of all parents in the sample with the exception of those few not interested in pre-school. Parents' previous experience with their other children affected their views of reactions expected on entry into pre-school. If they had already sent one child, then they felt more confident about predicting the younger child's reaction. Sometimes it was a case of having learned from bitter experience: 'I don't expect any reaction from him. My first son was dreadful – dreadfully upset. I had to stay with him for a term. Looking back I think I started him too early and he just wasn't ready.' This mother intended to wait until her child was four-years-old before sending him to a playgroup. In the meantime she felt she was preparing him through trips back and forth to the school which his brother attended and where the playgroup was held and run by local mothers. She felt he had become used to the place and to seeing his brother go there every day and come home later. The mother also ensured he had regular contact with other children apart from his brother since she felt this would help the transition into playgroup.

The parents' and children's familiarity with the setting had, therefore, a bearing on how the parents answered the questions regarding reaction over the first days. No reaction was expected from their children by 45 per cent of mothers while 27 per cent felt that any adverse reaction would be short-lived and mild. A few mothers thought their children would 'love it', 'welcome it with open arms' and generally enjoy pre-school as a means of playing with other children, toys and activities which they could not do at home. Parents expecting strong adverse reactions were most often found among those sending a child for the first time and 12 per cent thought their children would cling, cry or not want to leave them. A smaller number of parents felt unable to say how their child would react and here again they were usually found among those who had little or no previous experience of sending a child to playgroup or nursery.

The parents' judgment of their children's individual characteristics and behaviour also led them to predict that certain reactions would occur:

> At the moment I would expect her to be all right. She is not in a 'clinging' phase at present. I suppose she might be by the time she goes.

> She's a bit reserved, rather timid and may cling to me.

> He might be upset on the first day and on the second, third and fourth may not want to go at all. He always seems pleased to see me if I've left him. It's almost as if doesn't trust me to come back and yet I've left him less and he usually has his brother with him.

A minority of parents were consciously taking steps to prepare the child for playgroup or nursery. For example, one mother was making a practice of leaving her son for short periods with neighbours or friends so that he would be used to her leaving him and fetching him later on and also so that he would get used to other adults. Another mentioned leaving her child with relatives, such as grandparents, for similar reasons. One parent felt he was helping his child for the move into nursery by explaining what the nursery will be like; 'we are preparing her now and don't expect any reaction. We tell her she can play and learn and make friends. I hope this will be as we have told her.' This father had come to England a few years ago with his family and was making great efforts to learn about the culture and pass this on to his children.

Parents, then, expected less adverse reaction when the child was familiar with some aspects of the situation he was about to face. Familiarity with the actual surroundings, with other children and/or adults, or to being left on their own with other people, appeared to be of importance to some parents as a means of allaying the child's anxiety on entry into pre-school. Those parents who hoped that their children would start at a playgroup and then go on to a nursery anticipated no difficulties on entry into the nursery since, by then, the child 'would be used to going'.

Mothers seemed a little less certain of predicting how they themselves might feel on the first day of pre-school. A third thought they would take it as a matter of course and not be affected, whilst just under a third thought they would be slightly upset at first. Twelve per cent thought they would feel happy because their child was going somewhere interesting and they would perhaps have a little time to themselves. A higher proportion (21 per cent) believed that they would feel very upset. Individual previous experiences, number of children and familiarity with the nursery or playgroup again played their part as mothers explained their expected reactions. Sometimes they said they would feel upset because it was the first child to go away from them or they expected to feel nostalgic that the child was growing up and no longer a baby. Similar statements were however made by mothers whose last child was going into pre-school and by those who had only one child. They expected to feel hurt and upset and at the same time tried to laugh at themselves for thinking this because they believed that the pre-school would be a 'good' experience for their children. Parents' actual response to nursery entry is discussed in Chapter 5.

Parents were asked whether, in order to settle the child at pre-school, it would be best for them to stay or go immediately after taking the child. They were fairly evenly divided in favour of staying (48 per cent) and of going immediately (47 per cent). Mothers were therefore more likely than nursery and playgroup staff to see their early departure as beneficial; we saw in Chapter 2 (Table 2.4) that only ten per cent of nursery and four per cent of playgroup staff thought mothers should leave immediately. There seemed to be no clear differences between the two groups of parents that wanted and did not want to stay. Mothers appeared to opt for either course of action whether or not they anticipated their children being upset. In each case the mother felt she would be taking this action in the best interest of her child. Mothers who said they would like to stay with their children sometimes said they would stay only long enough to satisfy themselves that the child was settling in: 'I would stay a little while, not the whole morning, and would get her involved, get her to do something, then leave'. Some mothers said they would stay if it was a playgroup because this was the accepted practice: 'The mums do stay. Most playgroups expect you to stay the first morning, then it dwindles down to half an hour a morning. I should think that's the general practice.' But not if it was a nursery: 'I would stay with him at playgroup – they'd expect it. I wouldn't stay at the nursery. When I took my daughter to the nursery the teacher sat her on her knee, so I went.' The parents tended to say that they would do what they felt the staff expected them to do: 'I've always found it's best just to leave them. Mrs K at the playgroup advised leaving Tina (other daughter) and told me (later) she was all right five minutes after I left.' A number of mothers said they would ultimately take the advice of staff and this could override their own personal choice in the matter because they would not want to upset the staff.

Some mothers said they would not stay because to do so would prolong unnecessarily the inevitable parting or raise the child's expectations:

> Possibly it's best for me to go. I know she used to cry when I left her with people but, if you ignored it, she stopped.

> I would go immediately. A friend of mine stayed and after that the child thought she was going to stay all the time.

> It's best to leave him otherwise he'll never go on his own.

Some parents with children entering nurseries thought that the staff rather than the parent could cope best with the children:

> Leave them there and let teacher sort them out. If mum's there, it makes them worse.

> Parents can't help in this, they get emotional. It's best to leave the child with trained staff to deal with it. They know what to do.

A point brought up less frequently by mothers who did not want to stay was that by staying they would be defeating their own objectives, which included helping the children learn to be apart from them, to become independent and to become individuals in their own right.

Summary

In this chapter the home background and experiences of young children have been explored using information from interviews with 86 parents in two counties of southern England. A range of home environments, in social and economic terms, was represented in this sample. The majority of children, however, lived in family units of mother, father and one or more siblings and in adequate accommodation, usually with access to an outside play area. Although 30 per cent of mothers worked regularly outside the home the majority were at home during their children's waking day. There was little evidence of parents sharing the responsibility of their children equally and the traditional pattern of mother as 'housewife' and father as 'worker' predominated.

The children's most frequent excursions outside the home were on shopping trips, followed by visits to the homes of parents' friends and relations, while visits to parks or going for walks were, in comparison, relatively infrequent. The majority of children therefore spent a major part of their waking life in their homes with mother as their main adult companion. There were differences between mothers and fathers in the way they played with their children. The former tended towards quiet activities such as reading, colouring and playing with their children's toys or games while the latter tended towards 'rough and tumble' types of activities. Fathers had less time available to spend with their children and a fifth saw very little of them during the working week. Sixty-one per cent of fathers and 47 per cent of mothers played for less than an hour a day with their children.

There were differences between the girls and boys in the kind of activities they did at home. More boys than girls played frequently with construction toys, small cars and similar toys and more girls than boys played frequently with soft toys, dolls and push pull types of toys (such as prams and trolleys). This suggests that very young children will enter pre-school with established sex-typical behaviour and expectations.

Parents emphasized the importance of learning of a social nature, such as learning to share or to mix with others, in their answers to both open and specific questions. The majority of parents were, however, helping their children learn numbers (counting), nursery rhymes, colours and shapes. While 69 per cent believed they had a marked effect on their children's development, they appeared to undervalue their influence on their children's learning except over matters where they saw themselves as competent. Very few parents said they were helping their child learn to read, suggesting that they did not recognize that the many everyday activities they did with their children (such as looking at books and reading stories) were able to affect skills necessary for reading.

Parents were able to distinguish between the various forms of pre-school provisions. Much of their knowledge came from friends and relations. There was a marked antipathy towards day-care services. All but three parents wanted their children to attend a playgroup or nursery prior to school entry at five. Given a free choice of provision the majority would choose either a nursery, or a playgroup followed by a nursery. Overall, parents, in comparison with pre-school staff, saw less benefit to their children from pre-school experience and stressed its value as a preparation for later school life. They saw little personal benefit to themselves, e.g. in having more free time. They believed that nurseries encouraged social and educational development while playgroups generally provided opportunities for social interaction but lacked the teacher-trained staff found in nurseries. Playgroups were seen as having the advantages of offering the morning sessions which most mothers wanted and convenience in that they were closer to home. In addition playgroups were seen as catering for younger children than nurseries and many parents could not understand why playgroups in their areas had raised the minimum entry age from two-and-a-half to three years. The majority of mothers believed that their children needed the company of similar aged children by the time they were two-and-a-half years of age. Over a third of the children had only infrequent contact with other children and 40 per cent of mothers thought more contact was needed.

Prior to entry to pre-school most parents wanted to visit the nursery or playgroup with their children to observe what went on there; while two-thirds (of all parents answering questions on nurseries) and 56 per cent (of those answering questions on playgroups) wanted to also meet the staff members who would be in charge of their children. Parents expected less adverse reactions from their children when they were already acquainted with some aspects of the pre-school setting. Half the mothers thought they would be either slightly or very upset when their children went to nursery or playgroup for the first time. They were evenly divided over whether they should stay with, or leave, their children on the first few days. There was no pattern to their choice, that is, parents opted for either course of action whether or not they expected their child to be upset. The overwhelming impression was that mothers expected their own wishes to take second place to those of staff in the event of entry to pre-school. Staff therefore need to make their policy clear to parents if misunderstanding is to be avoided.

Having described the views of pre-school staff and those of parents prior to their child's entry, we now turn to children's actual behaviour on entry into pre-school.

CHAPTER 4

Entry into Nursery Class

In this chapter we follow 51 children through their first weeks at two nursery classes. After a description of the nursery classes involved we describe:

1. data collection – how the sample was obtained and the research instruments used;
2. general results from the Observation Schedules and Child Adjustment Questionnaire;
3. changes in behaviour in the nursery during the first term;
4. differences between children in their response to entry;
5. associations between children's behaviour after entry and their previous experiences.

Nursery A

This was a purpose-built nursery class situated in a redeveloped area of London. It was physically set apart from the infant school by a corridor and consisted of a large room with adjoining toilets and a second smaller room used for story time and quiet reading.

The large room was divided roughly into two halves. A carpeted area had a permanently laid out home corner, a book corner and topic table. Observations took place in the early autumn when the topic table contained a variety of seeds. Next to this was a small dramatic toy area consisting of a pictorial carpet printed with roads, trees and fields, beside which were toy cars, garages, zoo animals and a dolls' house. Tables and chairs were also laid out in this half of the room with various construction toys, jigsaw puzzles, Lego, etc.

The uncarpeted half of the room housed the messy materials like the painting easels, sand and water trays and plasticine and dough. All the glueing and sticking activities were restricted to this area.

This was an 80-place nursery with 40 children attending each morning and afternoon session. The younger children (three-year-olds) tended to be admitted into the afternoon session as the hours were shorter. It was staffed by two full-time nursery teachers, two full-time nursery nurses and a part-time NNEB student for two days a week. The children arrived at 9 am and were usually welcomed at the door by the staff. The reception hall and corridor where their coats were hung were fairly narrow which resulted in a bottleneck preventing easy communication between the parents and staff. A short play period followed in which the children were free to choose which activity they preferred from a wide range of toys and materials.

At approximately 9.20 the register was called. This took place in the small 'story' room where they were expected to sit still and encouraged to answer appropriately when their names were called. After the register the children were anxious to tell the nursery teacher their 'news'. She seemed to enjoy this conversation period and often took the opportunity of introducing a topic for discussion or reinforcing some of the nursery rules. This period was frequently terminated with a teacher inviting the children to look at the books, but very few of them took up this opportunity; they usually quickly filed out into the larger classroom or playground.

After an hour all the toys were cleared away and, as the tables were set for milk, the children were divided into two groups for story time. Either a nursery teacher or nursery nurse ran this period which lasted about 15 minutes. Several short books were read with the pictures held up for the children to see. Often a few nursery rhymes were added to fill in the time before a 30-minute structured session. This session varied from day to day. Once a week a member of the infant staff played the piano while the children sang or marched round to the music.

Sometimes the children played musical instruments and at other times they played team games. After this structured session they prepared to go home.

The afternoon session was very similar except that it was shorter with the half-hour structured play omitted.

In this nursery the responsibilities of the nursery staff seemed fairly clearly defined. The nursery teachers were very much engaged in 'educational' aspects, organizing the topic of the day and encouraging the children to perform various skills, while the nursery nurses had more of a caring and clearing up role.

Nursery B

This was a purpose-built unit housed on the same site as the main first school but separated by a playground. It was situated in a mainly working class area, but the percentage of middle class children attending this nursery was higher than for the London nursery.

The building consisted of a large room with various carpeted alcoves; one acted as a 'house area', another was used for register, prayers and group sing-songs, and one could be partitioned off in order that the 'rising' five-year-olds be given a formal lesson each day in preparation for first school. An alcove incorporated the entrance door and cloakroom. As in the previous nursery this area became congested with parents and children though, perhaps because it was rather more open, communication between the nursery staff and parents seemed easier and staff welcomed the parents of the new children and encouraged them to stay as long as they liked.

The main area in this nursery was devoted to equipment and toys. Each day a different selection of construction materials and puzzles were laid out on tables, though to some extent the children could take out whatever equipment appealed to them. In the centre of the room the large apparatus such as multi-purpose boxes, rocking horses and slides were situated. Children played on the floor with train sets, garages and cars and it was frequently difficult to walk from one side of the room to the other without disturbing a game or treading on a toy. (We were observing in January and February when it was too cold for the children to play outside, so no doubt the overcrowding would have been relieved later in the year.)

The children arrived for the morning session at 9.15 and played with the set out equipment until they were divided into two groups for register. During this time the nursery teachers held up milk rings, each with a child's name on. The children had to watch for the ring with their name, collect it and place it on a milk bottle. At milk time they had to find their own bottle. This was a fairly complicated procedure for newcomers, but most of them soon learnt to recognize their own name (see p. 40 in Chapter 2).

A free play time followed register but small groups of children were encouraged to wash their hands and drink their milk. This was not the formal group occasion as in the other nursery – here they were able to sit on the floor or bed while they drank and talked to their friends. The only rule seemed to be that they had to sit down until they had finished drinking or eating; in this atmosphere very little milk was actually spilt, and most children drank happily to the end of the bottle.

Most days when milk was over the children were free to choose their own activity though one day each week was devoted to music and movement in the main school hall. Each member of staff had ten children to supervise while they changed into plimsolls and stripped down to vests. Several of the newcomers found this a disturbing event and refused to take off their clothes or would not join in the dancing but sat at the edge of the hall and watched. The staff tried to encourage them, but did not force them.

Each day a member of staff led the children for a half-an-hour session. Various action rhymes and songs were introduced to the children, often with the aid of records. At the end of the morning all the children had to help tidy up before listening to a story. The parents arrived at this time which meant that a number of children missed the end of the story. The afternoon session was a repeat of the morning – both taking two-and-a-half hours.

This nursery was staffed by two nursery teachers and two nursery nurses, and, as with Nursery A, 40 children were enrolled per session. In contrast to the other nursery, there was no clear division of responsibility between the nursery teachers and nursery nurses. All were equally involved in the 'educational' components, helping and disciplining, though the teachers took charge of official matters like register and records and the nursery nurses supervised toileting, hygiene and milk drinking.

1. Data collection

The sample

As described in Chapter 3, the headteachers of the two nursery schools were approached for names and addresses of all the children due to start nursery the following term. The parents were interviewed (see Chapter 3) for permission to study their children and to gain valuable background information such as socioeconomic status, a description of the home environment, the amount of contact with other children, adults and siblings, parents' attitudes towards education and their perceptions of pre-school. We finished up with a sample of 51 children who actually started nursery school, and obtained background information on 33. Parents of the other 18 children could not be interviewed prior to entry because it was not possible to get notice of their entry in time.

We observed each child for his first 15 days (i.e. three weeks) and then returned three weeks before the end of the first term for a further five days of observations. It was fortunate that both nurseries staggered the entry for newcomers because it meant we were not faced with more than about five new children on any one day. The nursery staff helpfully put labels on each child so we could remember their names – this was for their benefit as much as ours. The average age of entry was 41 months.

In order to see if there were any differences between the behaviour of children in the two nurseries, a number of statistical tests were carried out on the observation data. Significant differences were found on only one variable – there was more adult/child contact in Nursery A(1)[1]. We therefore felt reasonably happy about pooling the data on children from the two nursery classes.

---

[1] All of the results reported in this chapter are based on statistical analysis, but in the interests of readability we have put actual results in Appendix 1. These results are referred to in the text by numbers in parenthesis.

Research instruments

1. *Observation schedules*

We devised two observation schedules. One focussed on children's contact with adults, other children and equipment in free play situations, that is, situations where children were free to choose whatever activity they wished, who to talk to and where to go. The second schedule was designed for the more formal adult-directed sessions such as story time, register, sing-song, music and movement, etc. The children were watched in strict rotation for a period of three minutes during free play and one minute in the directed sessions. Every ten seconds the most dominant behaviour of the 'target' child was coded and the number of time intervals within which children were observed in each category on each day was entered into analysis. The total record for each child varied from day to day depending on the number watched and the structure of the session. For example, if a long music and movement session was held on one day the length of time allotted to free play was reduced so our free play record for some children that day was shorter. We therefore expressed the data as ratios of time in a particular activity category divided by the total time that child was observed on that particular day. (A fuller description of the two observation schedules follows shortly and copies of the coding forms can be found in Appendices 2 and 3.) Percentage observer agreement for the free play categories taken together was 84.4 per cent. For the directed session this figure was 93.8 per cent. Inter-observer agreement figures for individual categories can be found in Appendix 4.

2. *Child Adjustment Questionnaire*

The nursery teachers in the two schools were asked to complete a 'Child Adjustment Questionnaire' for each of the 51 newcomers, ten days after admission. The answers that were given were an indication of how the children settled from the staff's point of view. The questionnaire was based on one devised by Chazan and his colleagues for the Schools Council Research and Development Project in Compensatory Education (Chazan *et al.*, 1976).

3. *McCarthy Scales of Children's Abilities*

All the children were tested with the McCarthy Scales of Children's Abilities. This was in order to ensure that they were all within the normal range, and to relate the scores to the home and behavioural data.

4. *The Home Inventory*

During the parent interviews described in Chapter 3, a 'HOME' Inventory was completed for each family. The inventory produces seven subscores which are designed to describe the home as a learning environment.

These instruments will now be described more fully.

1. *Observation schedules*

(a) *The free play observation schedule* – This schedule was concerned with five dimensions:

(i)   The child's activity
(ii) The child's toy type
(iii) Solitary or child/child interaction
(iv) Adult/child interaction
(v)   Apparent emotion of child

(i) *The child's activity.* Sixteen different activities were specified which were adapted and modified from those used by the Oxford Pre-School Research Group (Sylva *et al.*, 1980).

1. WATCH – Standing or sitting, watching or examining another child, adult, object or event, e.g. standing and watching a nursery nurse while she clears out the rabbit cage.
2. UNOCCUPIED – No constructive or manipulative activity with play material and apparently aimless, e.g. standing still, unoccupied and gazing round with an aimless look.
3. WAIT – Waiting for a specific action to begin, e.g. waiting for teacher to show how to draw round a template.
4. CRUISING – Moving and unoccupied. No particular activity occurring or intended, e.g. wandering round, appearing to be looking for something to do.
5. PURPOSEFUL MOVEMENT – Moving with an aim towards an object or activity, e.g. purposefully running to get on a pedal car in the playground.
6. CONSTRUCTIVE FINE – Manipulating small objects or material and paying attention to its properties, e.g. threading beads, building with Lego, doing jigsaw puzzles.
7. CONSTRUCTIVE GROSS – Similar to Constructive Fine but using large muscle movements, e.g. putting sand into a bucket or building with large building blocks.
8. NON-CONSTRUCTIVE – Non-constructive manipulation of material, e.g. destroying a sand castle that a group of children are trying to build, or deliberately splashing other children with water.

9.   3Rs – Any activity directed at books, reading or writing, e.g. tracing letters, looking at books, counting out loud.
10. ART – Activity involving painting, drawing, colouring, etc., e.g. drawing or painting at the easels.
11. LARGE MUSCLE – Activity using gross motor movements, e.g. running, climbing, sliding down the slide, cycling.
12. DOMESTIC – Activity not classified as play, e.g. toilet, hand washing, doing up shoes.
13. DRAMATIC – Activity with or without play materials involving any make-believe or role playing, e.g. making tea in the Wendy House or dressing up in nurses clothes and playing 'hospitals'.
14. GAMES WITH RULES – An activity structured by rules, e.g. card games, ludo, ball games.
15. INFORMAL GAMES – Play without any formal rules, e.g. pulling other children in a cart or pushing toy cars to each other.
16. SOCIAL NON PLAY – Any social contact which doesn't involve a game or activity, e.g. a brief social encounter by two children before they part and go their separate ways.

(ii) *The child's toy type.* The type of toy the child contacted was also noted. There was usually a relationship between the activities and toy type, but not always; for example, a bicycle which was classed as a large outside toy could be coded at the same time as large muscle activity or as dramatic if the child was obviously acting out some behaviour at the same time.

Toy types

1. LARGE TOYS – e.g. tricycle, pedal car, rocking horse, climbing frame.
2. DOUGH, SAND, WATER, PLASTICINE.
3. GLUEING AND ART TOYS – e.g. chalking, pencils, crayons, glue, cutting up material etc.
4. DRAMATIC – e.g. dressing up clothes, dolls, soft toys, Wendy House items.
5. SMALL CONSTRUCTIVE TOYS – e.g. jigsaws, Lego, beads.
6. LARGE CONSTRUCTIVE – e.g. train set, large bricks, pegboard.
7. SMALL DRAMATIC – e.g. farm and zoo animals, dolls' house, furniture, small cars.
8. BOOKS AND GAMES – e.g. books, card games, matching games.

(iii) *Solitary activity or child/child interaction*
PARALLEL – the child is close to another child, e.g. at the same table, but not interacting with him.
INTERACTION – any interaction or communication involving another child. It must show evidence of reciprocity of some kind.

SOLITARY – the child is on his own.

For every time period the size of group of the target child was coded. There were three sizes: pairs, small groups (three to five children) and large groups (six or more children).

We were also interested in whether the child initiated interaction, was responsive to others' advances, or if the interaction was a mutual one. We felt that as the child gained confidence he would be more likely to initiate interactions with other children. Unfortunately this proved difficult to code accurately and our reliability figures are low. These data were not therefore included in analyses.

We were able to record who vocalized in the interaction: if it was the target child, another child, or if they spoke together. A non-verbal interaction frequently occurred, particularly during sand and water play when two children were engaged in filling the same bucket or water wheel. They would often laugh happily together but no verbal communication occurred. (Vocalizations not directed to anyone were also coded ('vocalize to self').)

(iv) *Adult/child interaction.* We were interested in assessing the extent and type of contact soon after entry between children and the nursery teachers, nursery nurses and any other adult present. The five types of adult contacts with children were:

1. EDUCATIONAL – conversations directly involved in teaching the child some skill, or about the properties of something; for example, showing the children the seeds in the topic corner, naming them and drawing attention to their similarities and differences. Another example would be speech showing a child how to trace around the letters of his name.
2. HELPING – conversations that showed the child how to take his coat off, which peg to put it on, how to do up the painting apron, etc.
3. MANAGERIAL – conversations like 'Can you put that toy away and wash your hands now', or, 'It's time to go inside for a story now, so shall we put all the toys away'. It was used most when the sessions changed from free play to directed or at the end of a session when all the toys and equipment were cleared up. Our figures underestimate the quantity of managerial speech as we stopped observing children during transition from one session to another.
4. SOCIAL AND COMFORT – conversations like 'Hello Johnnie, did you have a good weekend?', or, 'Oh, you've hurt yourself, let's go and put a plaster on that'.
5. DISCIPLINARY –correcting or scolding a child.

As in child/child interaction, we tried to judge if the child initiated the interaction with the adult or if he was purely responsive, but again we found this difficult to judge reliably so have omitted it from our results.

We recorded if the adult vocalized to the child, the child vocalized to the adult, or if they vocalized together during each time unit.

The identity of adults close enough to converse with the focus child was also noted. There were five codes: teacher, nursery nurse, other adults, mothers, students.

(v) *The child's apparent emotional state.* We were keen to supplement the above categories by obtaining an account of children's emotional reaction to the nursery. We quickly discovered great problems in reliably coding something so subjective but pressed on with the following five categories: 'positive' behaviour was coded when the children were laughing or giggling over toys; 'distressed' was coded if the child was showing overt signs of being upset, e.g. crying, sobbing or clinging to an adult; 'aggressive' behaviour was coded for acts such as kicking, hitting and fighting over toys, throwing sand at another child; 'lost' was coded when children were obviously confused or bewildered; and 'neutral' was coded when the emotional state could not be described with any certainty. Despite the generally high agreement between observers (see Appendix 4), results from the study showed that 'neutral' was coded far more frequently than the other categories – indicating the general inability of this section of the schedule to categorize emotional state in a useful fashion. These data were therefore dropped from further analysis.

(B) THE DIRECTED SESSION OBSERVATION SCHEDULE

These observations were recorded every ten seconds, as in the free play schedule. We observed each child for one minute before going on to the next one. We again watched the children in strict rotation, and when they had all been observed once we began the list again. We reduced the observation time to one minute per child as the directed sessions tended to be of shorter duration than free play.

Observations were made of behaviour in the following five sessions directed by staff.

1. REGISTER, EDUCATIONAL TOPIC, NEWS – these were kept together because in the two nurseries we were concerned with they tended to occur in the same situation; the register was taken, then the nursery teacher introduced a topic and then listened to the children's news or items of interest for the day.
2. MILK, PRAYERS OR HYMN – again these two occurred at the same time. In one of the nurseries the prayer and hymn were followed by milk drinking.
3. STORY – this was given more importance in one nursery than in the other.
4. RHYMES, SONGS – one nursery had a prolonged singing and rhymes session taken by one adult while the rest of the staff had a coffee break.
5. MUSIC, ORCHESTRA, DANCING, GAMES

Two types of behaviour occurred in these five sessions: those when children were required to attend to the adult and those when attention was not required, for example when the adult was not directly addressing the children and her attention was focussed on something else (e.g. sorting out which book to read to the children or totalling up the numbers on the register).

The various behaviours we classified when the teacher expected attention were:

1. ATTEND – child sitting still and apparently attending to the teacher.
2. RESPOND APPROPRIATELY – if asked a question, or attempts to join in, e.g. nursery rhymes.
3. RESPOND INAPPROPRIATELY – not participating or attending to adult's questions. Inappropriate behaviour was defined in terms of the expectations of staff in a session.
4. INITIATE SPONTANEOUSLY – initiate statements relevant to the immediate conversation.
5. LOST – child looking round with an expression of bewilderment, as though he did not know what to do next. This was easier to code than in the free play observations because expected behaviour was more clearly defined.
6. INTERACTION – child interacting or interfering with another child instead of attending.
7. MOVE AWAY – child refuses to join in the activity, e.g. sitting on a chair at the edge of the hall and not participating in the music and movement session.
8. DOMESTIC – the child leaves the session for the toilet or hand washing.

Three behaviours were classified when the teacher did not require attention:

9. APPROPRIATE – the child sits quietly, waiting.
10. INAPPROPRIATE – the child becomes disruptive and interacts noisily with his immediate neighbours. In one nursery the children were expected to sit still and quietly drink up their milk – any deviation from this was inappropriate. In the other, however, milk was a less formal occasion with children sitting on the floor or bed together laughing and talking. In this case the only expectation was that the child had to sit down while drinking and eating; it became more of a social occasion and less like a formal meal time.
11. LOST – again the child looks bewildered by the whole experience.

Some of these categories were not classified frequently enough for statistical analysis on an individual basis, so several behaviours were merged together to produce the four categories that were used in the final analysis:

1. POSITIVE behaviour $(1+2+4+9)$ This was the sum of all the behaviours of an attentive and appropriate kind.

2.   NEGATIVE behaviour (3 + 6 + 10) This was the sum of all the be-
     haviours of an inappropriate or disruptive kind.
3.   LOST (5 + 11) This was the sum of all 'lost' behaviour.
4.   MOVE AWAY (7) This was as before.

2. *Child Adjustment Questionnaire*

This includes questions on whether the child showed signs of distress on
entry and if so of what kind; evidence of any other reactions; whether the
child was overtired, showed difficult behaviour, wet or soiled himself; a
rating of the child's concentration, attitude to staff and other children;
whether the child had formed any particular friendships with other children
and took turns and shared with them; a rating of the child's use of equipment
and any preferences the child showed for them; and a rating of the child's
behaviour in directed sessions.

3. *The McCarthy Test*

All the children were tested with the McCarthy Scales of Children's Ability
(MSCA). This was to ensure that they were all within the normal range, and
to relate the scores to other quantitative measures.

The MSCA yields six scales: Verbal, Perceptual Performance, Quantitative, Memory, Motor and General Cognitive. The motor skills results were
omitted as this measure did not seem relevant for our purpose. The general
cognitive score is arrived at by summing the verbal, quantitative and perceptual performance scores and standardizing the overall score. Our sample had
a mean of 106.2 and the individual scores varied from 88 to 130, so it was felt
we had children who were within the normal ability range.

Problems do arise when tests of this nature are given to children of this
age: 'The principal characteristics that interfere with satisfactory test performances are shyness, distractibility and negativism' (Anastasi, 1966). We
only encountered one case of shyness, where we felt the child obviously did
not do herself justice, so her score was excluded from the overall analyses.
There were also two highly distractible children but we were able to test
them on a few items each day before they lost concentration. 'Negativism'
can take the form of flat refusal or general unresponsiveness. Again this only
occurred with one child who stared at us blankly through all the verbal items.
The other children were anxious to 'play with our case of toys' and many
asked to be tested each day. We had been in both schools for at least four
weeks before we tested any of the children so the children had become used
to us by then and in general were responsive and uninhibited.

4. *The HOME Inventory*

During the course of the parent interviews (see Chapter 3), the Home Observation for Measurement of the Environment (HOME) Inventory (for years three to six) was completed. The schedule was devised by Caldwell and her associates in order to provide a simple quantitive measure of the home as a learning environment. The inventory is made up of 80 items which were the result of extensive pilot work and the application of research on child development. These items are grouped into seven subscores on the basis of their associations with each other. The subscores are as follows:

i. Provision of stimulation through equipment, toys and experiences – points are given if the home contains three or more puzzles, toys to learn colours, sizes, shapes, and numbers, building toys, ten or more books, etc.

ii. Stimulation of mature behaviour – this section includes encouraging the child to learn colours, rhymes, numbers, reading, teaching the child to put away toys after use and rules of social behaviour, etc.

iii. Provision of a stimulating physical and language environment – items in this section include whether the neighbourhood has trees, grass, etc., if the rooms are overcrowded, if the house is noisy with TV, radio, shouts of children, whether the mother uses complex sentence structures, correct grammar, pronunciation, etc.

iv. Avoidance of restriction and punishment – this section includes items such as mother does not scold or denigrate the child more than once during the interviewer's visit, whether the child is punished for spilling food or drink, or if the parent has to physically restrain the child.

v. Pride, affection and thoughtfulness – this consists of whether the parent encourages the child to relate experiences or takes time to listen to him relate experiences, if the parent structures the child's time with toys or activities, whether his art work is displayed in the house, whether the mother's voice conveys positive feelings when speaking to the child, etc.

vi. Masculine stimulation – a short section concentrating on whether the child spends time with father or father figure during the week, if he eats a meal with him, whether the child plays with a bike, a wheeled toy like a doll's pram, or a large muscle toy such as a swing, ball or climbing frame.

vii. Independence from parental control – the focus of this section is whether the child is encouraged to be independent or not; for example, does he choose some of his clothing, is he encouraged to dress himself, does he choose certain favourite foods, is he allowed to go to play in another house without a 'care-giver' accompanying him, etc.

Scores on these sections were summed to produce a total score.

Two qualifications concerning the schedule must be voiced. The first concerns the relatively crude way in which the home environment is quantified. For the most part questions are answered in terms of a yes/no format and clearly this does not allow a particularly subtle account to be made. The second qualification is that the schedule was devised in the USA and the generalizability of items to Britain is open to question. In defence of the HOME schedule, however, it should be mentioned that it has been extensively piloted to ensure its reliability and employed in research (e.g. Bradley and Caldwell, 1976; Elardo, Bradley and Caldwell, 1977). Moreover, on the question of generalizability, the items are clearly defined and unambiguous and it is our impression that they do apply meaningfully to Britain.

2. General Results from the Observation Schedules and Child Adjustment Questionnaire

We now discuss some general results from the instruments just described.

i. *Observation free play*

Children can divide their time in the nursery in three ways: they can be on their own, with other children or with adults. In addition, contact with other children can be divided into those that are in 'parallel' (engaged with the same material but not interacting) and those that are 'interactive' (the 'target' child responds to or initiates social contact). Table 4.1 presents mean totals for each week for these four possibilities. Over all four weeks children spent

Table 4.1: The mean frequency of 'solitary', and 'parallel' activity, child/child interaction and adult/child contact.

	Week 1	Week 2	Week 3	Week 9
Solitary	.417	.344	.359	.282
Child/child parallel	.319	.337	.305	.279
Child/child interactive	.260	.313	.328	.425
Total adult/child	.235	.219	.234	.174

Note: As described earlier, frequencies are based on the number of time intervals in which a behaviour occurred divided by the total amount of time a child was observed for that day. As a consequence the resulting mean ratios do not make an immediate impression on inspection. The reader will find most interest in comparing means.

significantly more time in solitary activities than either parallel (2) or to a lesser extent interactive contacts with other children (3). This is not to say that children may not be interested in other children or adults when coded in solitary activities – they may, for example, be thinking about contact or looking at others – but it does show that the bulk of children's time after entry is spent out of contact with children or staff. It is perhaps as well therefore not to exaggerate the extent to which the nursery environment places demands of a social kind on children.

The nature of child/child contact was explored further by noting the size of group involved. Children spent far more time over all four weeks in small groups (three to five children) than either pairs (4) or large groups (six or more children) (5). This owes much no doubt to the arrangements of nurseries into four or five tables, attracting small groups of children to the activities offered there. The relatively few number of contacts that occurred in pairs suggests that, at this point in their pre-school lives at least, children tend not to be specific in their choice of social partners.

Comparison of the amount of contacts newcomers engage in with other children and adults showed that other children are the favoured partners (6); over all four weeks adult/child contact occurred significantly less than even the strictest definition of child/child contact – 'interactive' ('parallel' contacts were excluded from this analysis). The relatively low frequency of adult/child contacts was a little surprising given that these results concern the immediate weeks after entry when one might have expected adults to occupy a more central role in children's activities. Other studies though (e.g. Bruner, 1980) have reported similar findings. Indeed Tizard, Philps and Plewis (1976) found that only in two per cent of observation time was staff/child interaction noted.

Table 4.2 shows the type of adult/child contact.

Table 4.2: Type of adult/child contact.

Adult/Child Contact	% of total time
Educational	2.5
Helping	2.3
Managerial	2.2
Social and comfort	1.7
Disciplinary	0.5
Total	9.2

Even when taken together, adult/child contact occupies less than ten per cent of children's time at nursery. As one might expect at this age level, disciplinary contacts were rare, and occurred significantly less than other categories (7). 'Educational', 'Help' and 'Managerial' contacts occurred with about equal frequency though in absolute terms rather low.

There have been some attempts in recent years to compare the roles of behaviour of teachers and nursery nurses in pre-school settings (e.g. Clift, Cleave and Griffin, 1980). No attempt was made in the present study to compare the two in any depth. It was found on the basis of the observation frequency data, however, that teachers contacted children more than did nursery nurses, and that both teachers and nursery nurses contacted children more than other adults, mothers or students (8).

Comparison was also made of the type of children's activity and toys used. These were coded irrespective of whether children were alone or with other people. The results are shown in Table 4.3.

Table 4.3: Percentage time by type of activity and toy type.

Type of Activity	% of time	Toy Type	% of time
Large muscle	19.8	Large outside	23.4
Constructive gross	18.6	Dough, sand, water	19.1
Dramatic	12.6	Dramatic	10.8
Constructive fine	12.1	Small constructive	8.8
Watch	11.6	Glue, paint, art	7.6
Cruising	5.0	Small dramatic	4.6
Art	5.0	Large constructive	3.1
Domestic	2.7	Books and games	2.5
Informal games	2.6	No toys	20.1
3 Rs	2.2		100
Unoccupied	2.1		
Wait	1.9		
Purposeful movement	1.9		
Social non-play	1.2		
Non-constructive	1.0		
Games with rules	0.6		
	101		

It can be seen that the four most popular activities were 'large muscle', 'constructive gross', 'dramatic' and 'constructive fine', with 'games with rules' occurring infrequently. This last result is not surprising considering that it depends on a fair degree of organized cooperation between children. The two most popular toy types were the large outside toys like climbing frames, bicycles, pedal cars, rocking horses, etc., followed by dough, sand and water – materials involving manipulation. Taken together these results suggest that children prefer the relatively low-level large muscle activities and materials that can be manipulated. Both can be relatively undemanding and perhaps afford initial security in a strange environment.

ii. *Observation directed sessions*

Table 4.4. shows the percentage of time children were coded in each of the four behaviours in terms of the five directed sessions. Data for the four observation weeks were summed for each child.

Table 4.4: Newcomers' behaviour in directed sessions.

	Register %	Milk %	Story %	Rhymes %	Music %
Positive	80.5	92.7	86.6	85.6	86.2
Negative	11.1	6.4	9.4	12.2	9.4
Move Away and and Lost	8.4	0.9	4.1	2.2	4.4

Children behave appropriately for the most part in all five sessions. 'Appropriate' behaviour was judged in terms of the demands of the particular session and the greater amount in 'milk' no doubt owes much to the relatively few demands and therefore the wider variety of behaviour that is acceptable. Conversely more inappropriate and disruptive ('negative') behaviour occurred in rhymes and singing sessions, most probably because children found some of the words and actions hard to learn, and in one nursery this session appeared to continue for rather too long. The relatively low amount of appropriate behaviour in 'register' owes much to children's attention wandering if their name is not being called; moreover the staff's attention was on the register or one child rather than the whole group, whilst in the other sessions she either had the support of the rest of the staff or was in charge of a smaller group and therefore able to attend to all the children present. This would also explain the higher amount of 'move away' and 'lost' in register. (These two categories were pooled here because of their infrequent occurrence.) Some directed sessions, therefore, were rather less prone than others to hold children's attention. This is worth considering if one agrees that newcomers to the nursery will become more easily and quickly assimilated if there is focus and continuity to events.

iii. *Child Adjustment Questionnaire*

One of the most important ways of helping the child over his first hurdle into pre-school is by taking him to visit the school before he starts so he can meet the staff and other children, and experience the classroom with all its toys and atmosphere (see Chapter 2). Staff said that 60 per cent of the sample had visited the schools before and most of these had been shown the classroom and teachers. Almost 40 per cent of these had older brothers or sisters attending the same infant school, so they were probably fairly familiar with the school before they began. This left 20 per cent of parents who had made a special effort to ease their child into nursery. However, 39 per cent of the children had not been near the nursery before they were sent on their first day. Sixty-one per cent of our sample had attended some sort of pre-school at least once before.

Staff were asked whether children showed signs of distress on their first days at nursery. The results showed that the majority were not openly distressed (71 per cent, i.e. 36 of the 51 children). However in response to another question, it appeared that most children were apprehensive or unsure on entry (73 per cent). However ten days after entry only six per cent (three children) were still showing signs of distress.

More generally, 15 (30 per cent) of the children were reported to show 'difficult' behaviour at some time over the first ten days after entry. Four children had difficulty interpreting instructions, three were defiant, four possessive, and three had screaming tantrums. Answers to another question showed that only three children had wet themselves during the first ten days and none of them had soiled themselves or been sick.

Children's immediate emotional response is only one aspect of their adjustment to the nursery. An important factor, and one essential to later school life, is the degree of concentration towards tasks and activities (Curtis and Blatchford, 1981). Teachers were asked about children's general concentration and 24 per cent were said to attend most of the time, 67 per cent were fairly good and attended for some of the time and to some things, and 16 per cent were poor, tending to flit from one thing to another. To another question, a similar proportion (18 per cent) found it difficult to attend in directed sessions like story, register, and singing, tending to move around or withdraw.

Another important aspect of children's first response to nursery concerns their attitude to the staff and other children. The results are shown in Table 4.5.

According to staff, children were mostly well-disposed toward them and other children with perhaps a slight preference toward themselves. Further information on children's social relations in the nursery was obtained by asking if children had formed particular friendships with other children. Three children had, 65 per cent (33 children) had to some extent and 30 per cent (15 children) had not. Moreover only 50 per cent of the children were reported to take turns and share with other children. Children may be well disposed to each other, therefore, but the degree of social integration is limited.

The interviews with nursery staff, described in Chapter 2, indicated that entry into nursery might be expressed in a preference for one item of play material. The majority of children in the two nursery classes showed no

Table 4.5: Children's attitude towards teachers and other children.

Child's attitude	to teacher	to other children
	%	%
Very positive and friendly	18.0	20.4
Positive on the whole	68.0	63.3
Shy, withdrawn, solitary	12.0	14.3
Hostile	2.0	2.0
	100.0	100.0

'to teacher' question answered for 50 children
'to other children' question answered for 49 children

preferences (78 per cent) whilst 22 per cent were thought to prefer one item of equipment or activity. In common with the observation data on play material preference (see previous section), the most popular were large outside toys (half of those children with one preference).

In summary, therefore, the majority of children were reported by teachers to have adjusted to the nursery in terms of a favourable attitude to staff and children and an interest in a variety of materials. These results, though, can only give a general account of entry behaviour because of the nature of the questionnaire type instrument used. There are also problems concerning the reliability of answers; not only are teachers inevitably forced to make subjective judgments about children but there are also limits to the amount of detailed observation they can make on each child in their care. It is for this reason that outside observers can produce a more reliable account, though, it must be remembered, one less informed by experience and day to day involvement with the children concerned.

3. Changes in behaviour in the nursery during the first term

Free play

Having considered children's behaviour on entry in a general way, we now discuss changes in behaviour over the first term. As we have said, the 51 children were observed for the first three weeks after entry and then for a week near the end of term. For each child we therefore had a record of the amount of time spent in each behavioural category on the schedule on each of the first 15 days and then on each of the five days near the end of term. On the basis of these data we could compare children's behaviour in the first, second, third and ninth weeks after entry.

First of all, though, data for each category in both the free play and directed sessions were inspected for each child and categories that were not approximately normally distributed and/or which occurred very infrequently were excluded from further analysis.

Perhaps the most striking results concerned developments in children's sociability, and these have been presented in Table 4.1.

Although more time was spent overall in solitary activity than in the 'social' categories (see previous section), solitary behaviour decreased after entry (9). In fact 'parallel' activities are hardly social in that they denote instances when children are in proximity to each other and contact the same equipment but do not interact with each other. These also decreased over the first term (10). The amount of contact between adults and children, already relatively low, also decreased by the ninth week (11). In contrast to these three trends interaction between children increased over the first term (12) and outnumbered parallel and solitary activity by the ninth week after entry. Clearly, then, sociability towards other children increases after entry at the expense of activity alone, in proximity to peers, or with adults.

We have already seen that children tend to stay more in small groups of three to five children than either pairs or large groups. What, though, is the situation over time? The relevant results are shown in Table 4.6.

Table 4.6: Mean weekly totals for the three grouping categories.

	Pair (2)	Small Group (3-5)	Large Group (6+)
Week 1	.232	.303	.033
Week 2	.231	.359	.051
Week 3	.258	.322	.057
Week 9	.259	.373	.072

The increase in the amount of activity in small groups was the most notable result (13). Interestingly there were no differences between weeks in the amount of child pairings, indicating again that specific friendships do not seem to play an increasing role after entry. Large groups of six or more children, though they occurred infrequently, did tend to increase after entry (14). These results show that the increase in social contact between children predominantly takes place in small groups and that these in turn increase after entry.

As well as the amount of time spent in different social situations the schedule also enabled coding of vocalizations. The results for these categories are shown in Table 4.7.

Table 4.7: Mean weekly totals of child to child, child to adult, and adult to child vocalization.

	Child to child vocalization	Child to adult vocalization	Adult to child vocalization
Week 1	.131	.049	.114
Week 2	.157	.048	.078
Week 3	.156	.057	.078
Week 9	.231	.032	.051

As would be expected from the foregoing results, contact between children either accompanied by, or through the medium of, vocalization, increased over the first term (15). Feldbaum *et al.* (1980), in a similar vein, found that oldstagers to the nursery talked with each other far more than newcomers. Adult/child vocalizations on the other hand had the opposite trend. Adult to child vocalizations occur more often than child to adult vocalizations, yet both decrease after entry (16). Considering the relatively low amount of adult/child contact in any case these results are a little troubling. That adults can help children is evident from results from the Oxford Pre-school Project – they found that adult presence tends to extend and elaborate children's play (Bruner, 1980). They also found that pairings between children facilitate elaboration in play yet we have already seen that these do not seem to play a central part in newcomers' activity either.

Table 4.8 shows where the reduction in adult/child speech takes place.

Table 4.8: Mean weekly totals of the five adult/child categories.

	Educational	Helping	Managerial	Disciplinary	Social and Comfort
Week 1	.023	.038	.029	.004	.029
Week 2	.016	.022	.017	.006	.013
Week 3	.031	.020	.017	.005	.010
Week 9	.031	.008	.021	.004	.009

Frequencies of each category are low and further statistical analysis was not thought advisable. Inspection of the data does suggest though that 'helping' and 'social and comfort' contacts account for the decrease. This is not surprising because over time children have begun to learn the nursery 'rules' and how to apply them, so 'helping' by adults would naturally decrease, and, after the first week, staff would not feel children needed their reassurance and comfort so much. 'Educational' and 'managerial' contacts did not seem to decrease, suggesting that adult/child contact that does take place, becomes more ostensibly 'instructional' in content.

Comparison over weeks in children's activity ('large muscle', 'constructive gross', etc.) and toy type did not produce conclusive results. We had expected to find changes during the first term in the first four categories – 'watch', 'unoccupied', 'wait' and 'cruising'. We had thought that these would decrease as children became more familiar with their surroundings and the equipment they could contact. However none of these showed any significant differences between weeks. There were significant differences between weeks in 'purposeful movement' and this had decreased by the ninth week (17). This is not as odd a result as may appear at first sight because it probably means that less movement was noted because children were spending longer at a particular activity.

One category – 'games with rules' – was coded very infrequently over all four weeks. It would seem that either the children were not developmentally ready for rule games or that these types of games were not available for them to play with. On one occasion a teacher formed a small group for a matching game involving shapes and colours with the children taking turns. It appeared to be popular amongst some of the children, though when the teacher left the group the children began to argue and the game soon broke up. This suggests that certain children would like to play organized card games, but the guidance of an adult is necessary. Small organized groups such as this would seem to be beneficial for the children as they encourage social learning, such as turn taking, and the development of speech.

Directed sessions

It has already been suggested that directed sessions can cause children the greatest problem of adjustment, most particularly because they require concentration to a person and a theme in a formal way that they are unlikely to be used to. We were interested in seeing whether behaviour in directed sessions changed after entry and with experience in such situations. The results are shown in Table 4.9.

Analyses were carried out on all five sessions for 'positive' and 'negative' behaviour and for 'lost' behaviour in register and story. 'Lost' behaviour in milk, rhymes and music and 'move away' in all sessions did not occur frequently enough for reliable analysis.

The only significant differences between weeks for 'positive' behaviour was in story (18) where it had increased by the ninth week; in the other four sessions 'positive' behaviour remained fairly constant. It was noticeable in the first weeks that some children were not familiar with books – sitting still and listening to a story was an unnaturally formal behaviour. One teacher kept stressing that 'You will like listening to stories when you've been here

Table 4.9: Mean weekly totals of positive, negative and lost behaviours during the directed sessions.

	Register	Story	Milk	Rhymes	Music
Positive					
Week 1	.809	.850	.927	.822	.839
Week 2	.785	.854	.924	.875	.872
Week 3	.806	.832	.929	.864	.872
Week 9	.826	.927	.930	.863	.869
Negative					
Week 1	.090	.085	.075	.103	.100
Week 2	.094	.101	.089	.116	.100
Week 3	.096	.118	.086	.128	.072
Week 9	.166	.069	.092	.142	.102
Lost					
Week 1	.097	.091			
Week 2	.121	.077	—	—	—
Week 3	.103	.062			
Week 9	.006	.010			

a little while' to a little girl who put her coat on ready to go home whenever storytime was announced. Such positive encouragement, along with the interest children begin to find in stories, no doubt explains the change of attitude.

Negative behaviour on the other hand increased in register by the ninth week (19). Thus register was the only session in which disruptive and noisy behaviour increased, possibly because children began, once their initial awe had subsided, to become a little impatient with a routine task in which very little of interest occurred.

'Lost' denoted an expression of bewilderment, as if children did not know how to behave or respond. By the ninth week children appeared to be more decisive in their behaviour because 'lost' behaviour decreased in both register and story (20). Interestingly this is accompanied by an increase of appropriate behaviour in the latter but inappropriate behaviour in the former. A surer response to staff controlled sessions, therefore, can express itself in ways at times acceptable and unacceptable to staff.

4. Differences between children in their response to entry

Up until this point, discussion has centred on the group of children as a whole. One essential issue, though, concerns differences between children in their behaviour on entry. We have already touched on this in the interviews with pre-school staff (Chapter 2) and the Child Adjustment Questionnaire results in this chapter, but it is now time to address the issue more systematically. What we required was a way of classifying children into groups on the basis of their similarity to each other on the range of observation, questionnaire and test measures used to assess behaviour on entry. We wanted to establish on the basis of the quantitative data whether there were different 'styles' of newcomer behaviour and in order to do this a statistical technique called cluster analysis was used.

Fuller details of the analysis used can be found in Blatchford (1982). For present purposes we want simply to describe the four styles that were identified. Analysis was based on the following variables:

Variables used in analysis of 'styles' of newcomer behaviour	*Instrument from which variable came*
General cognitive ability	Total score on McCarthy test
'Positive' behaviour in directed session	Observation (directed session)
Total adult/child contact	Observation (free play)
'Watch' + 'unoccupied'	"
'Constructive fine'	"
'Constructive gross'	"
'Large muscle'	"
'Dramatic'	"
'Solitary'	"
'Parallel'	"
Child/child interaction	"
Distressed or unusual behaviour	Child Adjustment Questionnaire
Attitude to staff and peers	"
Extent of concentration, taking turns, use of equipment, and behaviour in directed sessions	"
Friendship with other children	"

Variables from observation, test and questionnaire instruments were chosen in order to cover the range of data collected on the children. The particular variables used were selected on conceptual and statistical grounds as the most appropriate. Some variables which statistical analysis had shown to be highly associated were added together.

The four styles of entry behaviour were:

Group 1 'Distressed'

These children were generally poor in intellectual ability, in their attitude to teachers and pupils and in their concentration, use of equipment and behaviour in the directed sessions. Conversely they were more distressed on entry and exhibited more unusual behaviour. They also engaged in proportionately more large muscle activity which tended to be of a relatively undemanding and low level. As a group they were therefore rather lonely, with poor concentration and ability and were more distressed on entry.

Group 2 'Bright constructive – non-social'

These children were the opposite of Group 1 in having the highest scores on the test of basic ability and the lowest scores on the 'large muscle' activities. They also engaged in far more constructive (gross) activities. Conversely they were the most unlikely of all four groups to be passive onlookers ('watch' and 'unoccupied'). These children therefore showed no noticeable social preferences but seemed bright and busily occupied in constructive activities.

Group 3 Child relaters

These children were easily identified as being by far the most interested in contacting other children (child/child interaction) and in dramatic activities (which often occurred in the context of contacts with other children.) Conversely they rarely engaged in solitary activities or activities in 'parallel' to other children and had the lowest amount of contact with adults.

Group 4 'Adult relaters – constructive'

Like Group 3, Group 4 was easily identified in terms of their social preference, but in their case there was a strong preference for contact with adults. They also engaged in more constructive activities with puzzles, jigsaws etc. ('constructive fine') than the other three groups.

With the help of 'multivariate' statistical procedures it was thus possible to identify four styles of entry behaviour. One group of children were predominantly interested in other children and another in staff. The two other groups were similar with respect to having no strong tendency towards social contact with either adults or children but one was bright and used its time constructively while the other lacked concentration and application and was the more distressed on entry. It is as well to be cautious about these results, not the least because there is always a problem concerning the real existence of the groups produced by mathematical calculation. What we can say is that the groups are recognizable as styles of behaviour one observes in children at nursery class. Intuitively we all assess behaviour on a number of dimensions and so our everyday observation can tell us more than simple statistical analysis of only one or two behaviours. The advantage of the analysis presented here is that it can arrange in a precise way information on a number of dimensions. In fact the present analysis highlights the need for close observation of all behaviour of newcomers - a range of behaviours in different situations. A sensitive appraisal of each child and his or her needs depends on such an objective and comprehensive account. Unfortunately when one has very little time to stop and observe children in one's charge it is all too easy to base judgments and action on a partial account. Staff might find helpful the above variables, used in cluster analysis, as the basis of an assessment of children's adjustment to nursery. Adjustment could then be assessed, perhaps at weekly intervals, in terms of behaviour toward other children, staff and equipment.

5. Associations between behaviour after entry and previous experiences

One of the main aims of the study was that of establishing the extent to which behaviour after entry into nursery was related to experiences prior to entry. Data on past experiences came from the parental interviews. Questions used in analysis were: child's age, sex, the father's occupation (as a measure of socioeconomic position), the father's length of education, the mother's length of education, number of siblings, the position of the child in the family, the amount of time the mother devoted to playing with the child, the length of time the child played with siblings, whether the child attended pre-school, if he had a special playmate, how well he got on with other children and the amount of contact he had with other children. Total scores from the HOME schedule were also included.

Measures of behaviour after entry were: total scores for each child on selected free play categories; 'positive', 'negative' and 'lost' categories from the directed sessions; scores on questions from the Child Adjustment Questionnaire; and scores on the McCarthy test.

There were a number of associations between these two sets of data but it is important, before they are discussed, to stress the need for caution in interpretation. In brief, the reasons for this are that with a large number of statistical tests of association one must expect some to be significant on the basis of chance alone (one would expect 1 in every 20 - i.e. $p = 0.5$ - to be significant by chance). Another point that must be made is that any test of association is not informative about the direction of influence; in other words it does not tell us whether, say, more prior contact with other people caused a child to initiate more social activity at nursery, whether the child was active anyway and this brought about more contact in the home or whether behaviour at home and nursery are attributable to a third and unknown factor.

The safest policy is to search for patterns of association – where several results hold together to produce a coherent and relatively stable picture. Several such patterns were found, with the strongest being between scores on the HOME instrument and behaviour at nursery. With regard to free play, children from homes with higher HOME scores, and therefore from homes rated as providing more opportunities for learning, stimulation, affection, mature behaviour and independence, were more likely to engage in interaction with other children and 'constructive gross' activities, but least likely to be 'unoccupied' and in 'solitary' activities (21). The HOME scores were also related to behaviour in staff directed sessions, because children from homes with higher scores engaged in significantly more 'positive' (appropriate, responsive) behaviour and less 'lost' (bewildered, confused) behaviour (22). In keeping with American research (Bradley and Caldwell, 1976), HOME scores also correlated positively with a measure of ability; there was a significant association with the total McCarthy score and this appeared to be largely explained by the 'verbal' subcomponent (23), suggesting that linguistic home experiences are of most importance in behaviour at nursery. (Elardo, Bradley and Caldwell, 1977, found that HOME scores were significantly and positively related to children's linguistic development.)

There is evidence, therefore, that experiences in the home are associated with behaviour and ability from the very beginning of nursery attendance. The dangers of inferring direction of causal effects from correlational analyses has been mentioned yet such a strong pattern of association across a number of measures is suggestive of some influence from home to behaviour at nursery. One can say no more on the basis of correlational analyses. Only on the basis of research involving a controlled experiment can one make more definitive statements, though such research has seemingly insurmountable ethical and methodological problems.

Several other patterns of associations involved other variables from the parental interviews. A number of authors have reported sex differences in behaviour at pre-school. Smith and Connolly (1972) for example reported that girls spoke more with each other whilst boys made more and shorter social contacts. With regard to newcomer behaviour, Feldbaum *et al.* (1980) found that girl newcomers were more interested in teachers and boy newcomers were more interested in other boys. Perhaps as a result, girls seemed to take longer to become assimilated into the group.

Our own results showed that girls engaged in more 'Art' and to a lesser extent in more 'Constructive Fine' activities in free play (24). They were also judged by teachers in the Child Adjustment Questionnaire to have a more favourable attitude toward them (25). Boys on the other hand engaged in more 'negative' (unresponsive, inappropriate) behaviour in the directed sessions (26).

The fact that girls seem to enjoy doing puzzles, threading beads, Lego, etc. more than boys is interesting in the light of the findings, presented in Chapter 3, that boys played more often than girls at home with such construction toys. Perhaps the girls are more interested in them at nursery because they have had less experience of them at home, whilst the boys find other ways of occupying themselves.

That girls are more favourably disposed than boys to staff offers support to Feldbaum *et al.*'s findings (from the USA), though their other results concerning sex differences in behaviour were not replicated, nor Smith and Connolly's findings on the degree of interaction.

Garvey (1977) has this to say about the effects of birth order on behaviour: 'first born children spend more time watching and wandering about than do children with other siblings'. Our results produced a quite different picture. First born children in the sample were compared with children who were second, third, fourth or fifth born and it was the latter group who engaged in more 'watch', 'unoccupied' and 'solitary' activity whilst first born children engaged in more 'dramatic' activity (27). In a similar vein only children engaged in more 'dramatic' activity than children with brothers and sisters (28). Because of the qualifications mentioned earlier, it is as well to be cautious about these results, yet they are intriguing and, if valid, do warrant explanation. One possible explanation of the latter two results is that first born and/or only children are more likely to be thrown upon their own resources and the creation of an imaginary world and, in the absence of peers, are more likely to use adult behaviour as a basis for dramatic play. That children with siblings tend toward a more withdrawn and passive behaviour at first sight confronts the common sense view that such children would be more used to interaction and therefore more likely to seek it out in the nursery. These children, however, are predominantly the youngest in the family, and it is possible that by the age of three, with some of them at least, a set pattern of standing and watching older children may have developed. Younger siblings, for instance, can, by dint of inexperience, be forced out of older children's games. We cannot say on the basis of the present results whether such behaviour recedes after several terms in nursery and closer acquaintance with same-aged peers.

The final variable from the parent interviews that related to behaviour on entry was the amount of time mothers found to play with their children per day. Those who spent the most time tended to have children who engaged in more 'dramatic' activity and 'interaction' with other children. There was also a tendency for them to have children who engaged in less 'solitary' activity (29). It seems likely that mothers with only one child will spend more time with them than mothers who have several children to divide their time between, and so this is consistent with the results just quoted for position in the family. But it does suggest, also, that a more intense relationship with their mothers is likely to be reflected in a general social orientation toward other children in the nursery. The sheer quantity of social stimulation provided by mothers may be important but longer and more intimate social interaction is also likely to create conditions for a close attachment between mother and child (Schaffer and Emerson, 1964), and it is perhaps significant that Lieberman (1977) found security of attachment between child and mother to correlate with social competence with peers.

With regard to Lieberman's other results concerning a correlation between prior experience with peers and later peer competence, neither the extent of contact with other children, nor attendance at pre-school prior to the nursery (variables from the parent interview) were significantly associated with behaviour in the nursery (as measured by the observation schedules). However, those children whose teachers rated them in the Child Adjustment Questionnaire as being more likely to take turns with peers, tended to be those with prior pre-school experience (30) – offering only limited support to the effect of prior pre-school experience on behaviour after entry.

Summary

In this chapter we have focussed in a systematic way on how children behave during the first weeks after entry into nursery class. This was based on observation of children in free play and staff directed sessions, an 'adjustment' questionnaire on each child completed by staff ten days after entry, and a test of children's conceptual ability.

The observation data on free play were first analysed in a general way and it was found that children spent more time overall in solitary activities than in parallel or interactive contacts with other children, and contacts between children, in turn, outnumbered those with adults. The greatest changes in sociability after entry were increased interaction•between children, usually in small groups, at the expense of 'solitary' and 'parallel' activities and contacts with adults. There was a tendency for children to prefer 'large muscle' activities like running and tricycle or pedal-car riding, and especially with the large toys in the nursery.

Children's reaction to sessions directed by staff was mostly appropriate to the demands of each session, though there were more disruptions in register and this became more evident with time after entry. Perhaps because of staff encouragement, children became progressively more responsive in story sessions.

Teachers' assessment of how well children had settled ten days after entry showed that the majority of children were not openly distressed, though about a third showed difficult behaviour at one time or another. About a sixth of the children had poor concentration. Children were predominantly well disposed to staff and other children but there were limits to the social integration of peer contacts – limits evident in the number of children who had not formed particular friendships or who did not share and take turns.

Four 'styles' of behaviour after entry were identified. One group was mostly orientated toward peers and another to staff. The other two groups spent relatively less time in social contact but one group spent this time constructively, whilst the other group were less constructive, less bright, and more distressed on entry.

Finally, an investigation was carried out on associations between children's reaction to the nursery and their previous experiences. The strongest set of results involved the HOME schedule and showed that children from homes rated more highly as 'learning environments' tended to engage in more peer interaction and appropriate behaviour in directed sessions, score more highly on a test of cognitive ability, and engage in less unoccupied, solitary and inappropriate or disruptive behaviour in the directed sessions. Other variables that seemed to be associated with nursery behaviour were the sex of child, position in the family and the amount of time mothers found to play with their children at home prior to entry. Further implications of these findings will be discussed in Chapter 7.

CHAPTER 5

Four Case Studies of Children

In this chapter four children are described with the intention of conveying the experience of entry into nursery against the background of home and family circumstances and each child's individual characteristics.

The four children were chosen partly on the basis of the completeness of information available for each and partly for the way they illustrated the different reactions to, and experience of, going to nursery class for the first time. Each study draws firstly on information obtained during interviews with parents prior to and following entry, and, secondly, on detailed notes taken every day. In contrast to the systematic observational data these notes were not used for quantification but aimed to capture more of the immediacy and character of behaviour as related to the situation within which it occurred.

Interpretations of observed behaviour can be seen as subjective to the extent that these were informed by the observer's understanding of the child's activities in the context of the total situation: that is, having regard to information available about the child at home and at school. Each study is arranged in a similar manner, providing sections on the child's background, the period following entry, and a section for summary and comment.

Neil

Background

Neil entered nursery straight from home at the age of three years and 11 months. He was the youngest of five children living with their parents in a well-cared-for terraced house. Neil was also the only child from his mother's second marriage and his two half-sisters and two half-brothers ranged in age from nineteen to ten years. His mother thought of him as the baby of the family and considered that she, his father and the other children tended to 'spoil him rather'. Neil's maternal grandmother lived in a nearby flat on the same council estate, was a frequent visitor to his home and he himself, 'being a wanderer', often went to her home. His mother said, 'sometimes he seems to go a thousand times a day. He tells her I've made a cup of tea for her and brings her back or will stay and play. He sees as much of her as he does of us.'

One or other member of the family would take Neil to the local shops every day, but he disliked public transport and had only just got used to going by bus to the town and preferred not to go on major shopping trips. The family did not have a car but Neil's father was a lorry driver and he enjoyed helping Dad clean the lorry or held tools while repairs were under way. When indoors his favourite occupation was watching television, which he was allowed to switch on himself. He watched all kinds of programmes, from those for young children to those more suited to adults. He had books at home but did not enjoy looking at them much. His mother did not read to him, nor his father, though occasionally his youngest sister did. Neil's mother said that it was difficult to keep his concentration for more than a few minutes, that he tended to scribble in or tear books, and for this reason he had not yet been allowed to have books from the library.

While Neil's home environment was rich in terms of resources – there were all manner of toys, including a large rocking horse such as that found in a nursery – he spent much of his time playing with toy cars, playing in the garden or playing on his tricycle near his grandmother's flat. He knew few children of his own age and when he played with those 'over the flats' he often came back to complain to his mother that they had taken his toy cars or would not let him play with them. His mother played very little with him except for what she termed 'silly, stupid games' which involved running around or rolling on the floor. Very rarely she might make up a story to tell him. She thought he was bright for his age but she had little regard for education. She believed that raising the school leaving age to sixteen was a mistake since 'they ought to be able to leave at fifteen and get a job'. She thought that since she rarely left him with anyone other than a family member, and because he was 'given in to whenever possible', Neil might be upset on entering nursery. Her own attitude towards the nursery was ambivalent and she had put his name down at the suggestion of a relative; none of her other children had attended the nursery. She was not sure she really wanted him to attend and she said that Neil was not looking forward to starting; if he did not settle she was prepared to take him away.

Entry into nursery

On the first day Neil and his mother looked apprehensive on entering the nursery. He looked down at the ground, sucked his fingers and stayed close behind his mother. She came into the nursery with him and attempted to interest him in different play materials on the tables. One teacher raised her eyebrows at the other teacher in recognition that Neil's mother was 'feeling it a bit' as she put it later and was quite happy for the mother to stay as long as possible. On the second day the grandmother also came and hovered around near her daughter and grandson. After a few minutes the grand-mother whispered to our observer, 'I think I'll creep out now before he sees I'm going', and left the room. During the first days, once Neil left her side, Neil's mother also left the nursery. He did not cry on the first, or subsequent days, though on the third morning he spent a long period looking out of the window watching the path that led from the nursery to the school gates. On several days he brought a toy truck to school from his home but it was clear that the nursery staff did not approve of this. The second day he brought it, it was put on a shelf as soon as he left it on the floor, 'so as it will be safe, Neil'. The truck caused a few problems since Neil hung on to it while other children thought it belonged to the nursery and tried to play with it; also, during directed sessions play materials were supposed to be cleared away and Neil did not like parting with it. On the other hand it seemed to provide him with some sense of security, and served as a source of comfort during the first difficult days. Neil's mother fetched him early on the first day and he looked pleased to see her, ran to fetch his coat and was out of the door as quickly as possible.

Over the first week Neil's behaviour alternated between periods of sullen-ness, where he would look at the ground or furtively glance around him while sucking his fingers, and periods of boisterous activity. On the first day, although initially showing apprehension, he appeared to be self-confident. He approached other children to play on the large wooden boxes and followed instructions to wash his hands and to sit in the corner for register and story. He made no response to his name in directed sessions and did not join in any group actions. He fiddled with his shoelaces and constantly looked around at the observers. He sat with his back to the teacher taking the session and faced the children, watching them as they enacted rhymes and songs.

On the second, third and fourth days, Neil began ignoring instructions from staff and persisted in continuing his activities after the piano played (the signal for directed sessions to begin). Our observer noted:

3rd day
2.15 Neil wants two boys to give up the garage and cars to him. He hits one boy. The nursery nurse says he must not hit others and sorts out the dispute over Neil's car and the school's cars. He listens to her, then goes with the other boys to fetch more cars from the box. They then all play with the cars and garage.

2.38 Shouts loudly during rhymes. Also pokes Paul on the head and face while making silly faces at other children.

He was ill-mannered during milk sessions, began to kick other children and would try to go back to play before finishing his carrot or apple. Tempers became a little frayed and a minor battle of wills occurred between Neil and the nursery assistant supervising milk-times:

4th day
1.25   Playing at water tray. Tries to take things off the other children, e.g. a bottle and a toy shark. Looks around at other children and watches observer. Stops playing when the music starts. Hangs up apron and goes over to corner, stopping on the boxes to play as he goes. First sits on the bed then jumps onto the floor. Does not attend during register and looks at other children rather than teacher.

1.48   Sits on bed to drink milk. Swings feet and kicks boy sitting on the floor. The boy moves away.

1.56   Swinging feet again. Nursery nurse says 'Keep your feet to yourself' after he kicks someone else. Neil says 'I don't want no more' – he has a mouthful of carrot again. She tells him to finish eating it. 'It won't go down.' 'That's because you put too much in your mouth, swallow it.' 'Can't, I can't eat no more.' He keeps repeating this while the nursery nurse waits for him to swallow the carrot. He gets up to wander off. 'Neil, sit still.... Come on they've all emptied their mouths and are going off to play.' Later Neil says to nursery nurse 'I've done it' and is rewarded: 'Good. Good boy, off to play'.

Such behaviour persisted into the second week:

5th day
1.42   Tries to play on the boxes when he should be washing his hands for milk. Then onto rocking horse.

1.46   Told by nursery nurse to wash hands.

2.00   'I don't want no more' – the carrot again. He is laughing at nursery nurse, making a game of it. He is allowed to play with large Lego while finishing carrot. Holds the bricks so others can't get them. Then another boy takes the bricks but Neil laughs saying 'I got a piece', holding his hand behind his back.

2.30   Made to sit directly in front of teacher so that she can 'keep an eye on him'. Later on he fidgets, trying to lie down on the children sitting near him. Hits girl next to him who had also lain down.

6th day
1.12   Playing with fort and soldiers with another boy. No conversation.

1.38   Finds his name ring after register but pushes several children out of the way to get there before them. Kicks girl sitting on floor in front of him.

2.20 Told to sit nearer nursery nurse and get off bed. Immediately talks to boy next to him, then hits him. Nursery nurse says 'bad boy' and Neil hits him again. Other boy moves away from Neil and Neil begins shouting 'I want to go wee wee'. He is ignored, then told he may go in a minute. He is then told 'You say please may I go, Neil'. He continues to fidget after going to toilet. He is inattentive and interrupts story-teller saying, 'I want to tell you something!'

On the seventh day he kicked others less often and seemed to be making an effort to participate in the group sessions; he joined in a rhyme at the end of the story session and listened seriously for short periods. After this day he was away for his birthday and then had 'flu' and did not return for two weeks. On his return he seemed subdued and apprehensive, as on the first day. His father and mother brought him in but did not stay for long. He looked bored and miserable. His father brought him again the next day and the teacher suggested one of the other boys should take Neil around the nursery. He behaved reasonably well all afternoon. The following day he did a puzzle with another boy and by the fourth day of his return the observation notes reflect his generally more cooperative behaviour.

1.20 More sociable, showing willingness to share and trying to help others. Offers helmet to another boy. No noisy outbursts.

2.15 Playing with Lisa; seen with her on several occasions.

3.00 Pulls girl over by the legs. First naughty incident today.

Since his return he had given up drinking milk but continued to sit down to eat an apple or carrot without fuss. He attempted to join in the rhymes and was generally more sociable with the children. By the final week of observation he seemed to have been absorbed into the nursery and had a number of contacts with boys with whom he entered into dramatic play involving 'firemen and engines' or 'marching' games. He seemed to like one girl in particular but she generally ignored his attentions. Neil was by now showing far more variety in his activity, doing puzzles, hammering pegs, playing in the sand, looking at books and painting.

Summary

During his first weeks at nursery Neil adapted not only to an unfamiliar routine but also to standards of behaviour not previously required of him. From his home life one might have predicted that he would be fairly inept at social interaction with other young children and that he would be confident with other adults in his expectation that they would do as he desired. This, largely, was our impression of his behaviour over the early days. He had no difficulty in interpreting the routine of the nursery since on the first day he rapidly followed signals from staff and other children over the matter of stopping play at the appropriate times. It seemed that on subsequent days he deliberately displayed his worst behaviour in order to test the adults present. Once he discovered that this behaviour was not to his advantage – for example prolonging the eating of carrots meant less time to play or that other children avoided him if he kicked them – he appeared to curb his aggression and produce behaviour which was more acceptable to the rest of the nursery.

At home after entry, however, life continued more or less as usual. His mother thought that, if anything, he had become cheekier and more selfish. It seems possible that Neil's behaviour at home served to reassure him that he was still of central importance to his parents and in time this reaction would pass. One change wrought by his attendance at nursery was in the attitude of his mother towards pre-school. She praised the staff's handling of his early days and said:

> With the others (older children) they were all small together. Him being on his own, I think it's wonderful for him to have company.... He has to learn to share down there as he's spoilt at home. Down there he learns everything is not his. So for an only child or the baby of the family the nursery is a good thing.

However, her attitude towards the value of education in general seemed not to have changed. She did not view the pre-school environment as either advancing or enriching her son's educational attainment but persistently emphasized the social experience from which she believed her son was benefiting.

Laura

Background

Laura had attended a playgroup regularly for six months from the age of two years. Her parents then moved house and did not try to find another playgroup for her, preferring her to wait until she could enter the nursery at the age of three years and nine months. Her home was a four-bedroomed house furnished comfortably in a modern way, and situated on a small private estate. Her paternal grandmother lived in the home and Laura spent a great deal of time with her during the day from early morning, when she would creep into her bed, until bedtime when the grandmother might read stories to her. Laura's mother had, until the birth of her second child (when Laura was three and a half), worked in the afternoons and Laura had become greatly attached to the grandmother who had looked after her. Two aunts took Laura out with them quite frequently, one having a son the same age as her. Laura's mother said that the children did not get on very well, Laura tended to be 'bossy and aggressive' while her cousin was 'quiet and shy'. With her own baby brother, however, Laura seemed to be coping well and her parents said they had made every effort before and after the birth: 'to involve her in looking forward to the baby and to do our best to include her so that she would not feel left out'. Laura had a very good variety of toys at home and particularly enjoyed jigsaw puzzles, painting and activities involving crayons and pencils. She also spent as much time as possible in the garden on her 'scrambler' bicycle and played with her small cars on most days. She played with water quite often but not playdough, plasticine or sand. She also liked playing pretend games with her dolls and her small toy tree house, cooker and vacuum cleaner. Laura's mother said: 'She plays with anything really and tends to amuse herself. For example, I have a button box and she spends a long time getting bits out of that.' Laura's mother played with her during the day, usually snakes and ladders or drawing or making pastry and dusting. Her father worked shifts but when he was at home he spent a little time playing games with her or looking after her. She was therefore used to the company of interested and encouraging adults prior to entering nursery but had relatively little recent contact with young children. This was a major reason for wanting to send her to nursery since her mother felt that she needed 'the right sort of company as there are too many grown-ups around her recently'. Laura was looking forward to nursery and her mother did not expect any adverse reactions on entry.

Entry into nursery

These expectations were realized on the first morning. Laura came with her mother but left her side almost as soon as they came in. A sample of the observer's notes for Laura's first day give an indication of how well she settled in.

1st day
9.20   Mother talking to teacher and Laura goes off to play – looks quite happy on rocking horse. (Mother left after few minutes.)

9.30   Laura at table with two others, drawing. Sits contentedly crayoning round animal template.

9.40   At easel with paints. Doing painting on her own. Nursery nurse admires her painting. After finishing Laura walks around and talks to other children and the nursery nurse.

As the morning progressed Laura continued to show her sociable nature by chatting to children during milk and also during the nursery rhyme session, where she discussed another girl's hair bunches but joined in with words and actions when the teacher regained her attention. She favoured the horse on this first morning and sat rocking vigorously, and frequently talking to herself, the horse or to imagined others. She left the nursery happily with her mother. This confident, sociable behaviour continued in the following days and Laura rapidly adapted to the nursery routine. She responded promptly to the music after noticing that other children stopped playing and moved to sit on the mat ready for register and other directed sessions. Laura seemed to talk most of the time – to herself if there was no one else nearby – though she listened fairly quietly during story and similar group activities. On the third day she volunteered to be a 'mouse' when the class was enacting a nursery rhyme and appeared to be competent and mature when responding to adults. With children she tended to take charge, as the observer recorded:

4th day
10.05   Doing puzzle with boy – he started it but she has taken over completely and won't let him do it. Still talking. Keeps saying 'No, that piece goes there'. The other child stands by her, trying to do it but not getting much chance.

Generally Laura seemed to be independent and liked doing things for herself; when she could not manage she tended not to ask for help and on these occasions she simply stood looking lost and unsure. For instance, after the first PE session in the hall at the main school, when it was time to dress, she stood holding her cardigan until eventually a nursery nurse helped her to put it on. Then another adult helped her take it off again as she had not yet put her dress on. On another occasion – an 'orchestra' session – she looked very worried as the older children made a noise with their instruments while waiting to begin. Once she had been given some bells and begun shaking them she looked much happier.

During her second week Laura showed signs of being unsettled in comparison with her behaviour in the first week. She still talked most of the time but it was becoming more noticeable that other children frequently ignored her approaches. She began wandering off at inappropriate times, for example when she was supposed to be changing for PE, and began playing with toys when supposed to be washing her hands or drinking her milk. On her seventh day at nursery she was very unsettled, wandering around, still chatting but being largely ignored, and did little in the way of constructive play. Her main occupation when not wandering was dramatic play in the wendy house on her own or in parallel (i.e. no social interaction) with other children. On one occasion she looked tearful but no incident was noted that might have caused this. The next day he mother spoke to the teacher in charge before the session saying that Laura had complained of being bullied and had not wanted to come to the nursery that morning. The teacher and the rest of the staff were surprised and unable to account for Laura's complaint, believing that she had settled down extremely well and was apparently happy to be there. An extra effort was made over the next days to watch for any friction arising between Laura and other children but no specific difficulty appeared to occur. She stayed at the nursery that day without looking unhappy when her mother left. She spent a long time playing in the sand tray and this was the first time she had settled to any activity for that length of time. In the Wendy House she showed signs of verbal aggression when wanting items with which other children were playing.

A weekend intervened and during her third week Laura again seemed relatively settled. Interaction was spasmodic and she was less talkative; she spent less time aimlessly chattering to imaginary people or children who were not listening or responding to her. Perhaps as a result of this quieter behaviour Laura seemed lonely and set apart from the other children; previously her failure to establish interaction had been somewhat masked by her bright chatter. She seemed to look more lost but still persisted in doing things for herself and did not ask anyone for help. She befriended another new girl during this week whose behaviour had been consistently solitary, silent and watching. Laura persisted with her kindly attention, choosing to sit near her, sometimes chatting, but often initiating non-verbal contact (holding hands, patting, smoothing the girl's hair). Eventually the girl no longer shied away from her and even gave the occasional encouragement or half-smile.

In the final observation week, nearly two months later, Laura was seen to have established relationships with the other children. She was again talking quite frequently, with the difference that others now responded. Her friendship with the other new girl had persisted and they were seen to be walking around holding hands. Laura appeared to be the guide and the other the follower. During directed sessions she was attentive and responded well with appropriate words, songs and actions. She cooperated well when playing with other children, sharing toys amicably and looking as though she enjoyed the nursery. She took part in a variety of activities and was seen to take drawings to show a teacher as though needing reassurance and approval. Her dramatic play in the wendy house was continuing though more often in partnership with others. Occasionally she pretended to be teacher and sat 'reading' a book to other children, using her imagination to make a story from the pictures or retelling a familiar rhyme.

Summary

Initially, Laura's experience of nursery was fulfilling. Unlike Neil, Laura obviously wanted to be part of the nursery and a constructive attitude towards the idea of pre-school had been fostered at home. Although she had had few recent experiences of playing with other young children, Laura appeared to have remembered her former playgroup and was ready, it seemed, to take up where she had left off. Her behaviour was mature and her understanding and vocabulary advanced when compared with others at the nursery and this, combined with the fact that for almost a year her main company had consisted of adults, may have helped create the slight setback which occurred during the second week. Laura's initiatives and persistent chatter appeared to put other children off and it seemed that Laura's conversational expectations were inappropriate for her peer group. Since she was of a relatively independent nature and used to amusing herself she did not turn to other adults for interaction nor did she complain to them of bullying. It was her grandmother who had finally elicited from her the reason why, during the second week, she had become unhappy at home and had not wanted to go to nursery. No particular incidents were noticed, but it is probable that just one unpleasant experience, unseen by others, was enough to upset Laura because she was already experiencing some social difficulties with children and unsolicited support and interest from helpful adults was generally less forthcoming than that she was used to at home.

In general, Laura came to the nursery adequately prepared and she settled down well in a short period of time. The only cause for concern in her case was that the nursery might not provide enough stimulation in educational terms. On arrival she was already, when compared with her peers, well behaved, sociable, verbally advanced and had learned and heard many rhymes and stories at home and playgroup; the nursery would need to provide suitably advanced experiences if she were to progress further. At the end of term her mother expressed certain misgivings on the educational aspect of nursery; she would have liked more information on the nursery's aims and methods, particularly on their policy for reading because at home Laura was showing interest in words, as well as pictures, and her mother was unsure how to help her or whether the nursery would approve of her teaching her to read at home. She was advised to approach the staff with her questions.

John

Background

John was an only child, though his mother was expecting her second about three months after he was to enter nursery. She was anxious for him to go to nursery well before the baby was born so that he would not feel he was 'being pushed out' because of the new baby. John had a close relationship with his parents, and his mother's brother (John's godfather) was a frequent visitor to their comfortable three-bedroomed home on the outer edge of the nursery catchment area. At home John played mainly with his bicycle, pedal car and football and liked playing in the small garden whenever the weather was fine. Indoors he enjoyed playing with his cars and garage and puzzles. He would dress up as 'Batman' and on most days tried to draw or scribble. Occasionally he played with plasticine and liked to play with pastry whenever his mother made some. He also 'washed up' and tried to help his mother around the house.

John was three-years-and-eight-months-old on entry to the nursery and had attended a playgroup for five months from the age of two and a half. For the past nine months he had been at home with mother because the playgroup had closed down and she had been unable to find another near enough. John's mother would have preferred him to start at the nursery nearer the age of three but there were no places available and he had to wait. She thought that at playgroup he had learned to play with other children and had opportunities for messy play, but on the whole the nursery would, she believed, provide far greater educational facilities because of the trained staff and the variety of equipment they had available. She expected him to settle down well but thought he might cling on the second or third day.

He'll be very good the first day. The second day or the rest of the week he will probably cling but not at first. He won't let other boys see him act the baby. I'll stay if he wants me but I'll make it clear that it is only a one off thing – so that he doesn't expect me to stay all the time. He knows what to expect from being at playgroup and he is happy about nursery and looking forward to it.

Entry into the nursery

1st day
9.20   John arrives with his mother. She comes into the room a little way and says to him: 'Are you going to be a good boy?' John nods and gives her a goodbye kiss. Teacher comes up and says to some older boys nearby: 'Show him where the toilets are, boys.' John goes off with them, leaving his mother and teacher. After a chat with the teacher his mother leaves.

9.38   John stands watching the teacher, then moves towards one of the children playing on the floor with the train set. He follows this boy to the wooden climbing play cubes and stands near, watching him go in and out of the boxes before joining in.

10.00   Still in the boxes with several older boys. He has not yet spoken to them but is looking happy. Teacher speaks to him as she does his shoe lace up. Boy speaks to him and he responds by laughing and going back into the boxes. Shortly afterwards John starts to talk to Andrew (his original contact at the train set). John wants him to go and see 'something exciting' in the playhouse. Andrew does not follow John, who gets to the playhouse before realizing this and turning back towards the boxes.

He continued to play on the boxes, jumping off them and sliding down the attached low wooden slide. When the music played to signal register he wrongly followed Andrew into the small room but came out to the correct group on the mat when asked (the register session was split into two groups). After milk he returned to the boxes with other boys, laughing and running up and down the slide. He later watched the rabbit for a time. During the story he looked bored but generally paid attention and only occasionally fiddled with his shoe laces. He attempted to join in the last line of the last rhyme of the session. Towards the end of the first morning John jumped off the boxes without looking and landed on Andrew's legs. Andrew moaned at him for doing it and went into one of the boxes where he cried for a short while. John looked stunned but did not say anything to Andrew. He went off to the playhouse to fetch a hat. For the rest of his first session he played on his own, making dramatic gestures to himself whilst wearing the hat, and cruising around and watching other children at play. He greeted his mother with a cheerful 'Hello Mum'. She helped him on with his coat and they left.

This first day established the pattern of John's early weeks at the nursery. His mother brought him each day but left as soon as she had helped with his coat and kissed him goodbye. She often gave him a few pence to put in the nursery fund box before leaving. Although he had found a group of older boys to play with he seemed very much on the periphery of the group. He made a number of initiatives, asking other boys to follow him, but these approaches were rarely taken up and he continued to play his own dramatic games in the middle of theirs. He consistently moved toward the playhouse each morning to find a helmet and this behaviour was still taking place when we observed him towards the end of term.

On the third day one of the boys in the group to which he had attached himself said to him, 'I'm sergeant, you be the soldier', and a dramatic sequence began where the boys, all wearing hats, began marching around. By the fourth day he had mastered the nursery routine, had learned to recognize his name on the milk rings, but looked extremely bored during directed sessions like story and register and fidgeted a lot with his shoe laces. He also sat up on his heels instead of cross-legged and was told twice to sit down properly and also, 'Those children who undo their laces in songs don't get to go out to play on days when it is nice enough to go out'.

For John, like many children, the directed sessions seemed to create the most obvious problems for adjustment. Children have simply not realized what is basically required of them by staff: they are expected to attend to one person and one theme for a specific length of time. The child finds it difficult to recognize that the theme – whatever it might be – tends to have a beginning, middle and end.

John tried to help at packing-up times by putting materials away and by the second week had begun joining in most of the rhymes at the beginning of each directed session, though he then grew bored and would start to nudge his neighbours or pull faces at them.

During the third week John continued to play near the same boys he had been near on the first day. Andrew was, by now, tending to follow John around and would attempt to participate in John's games. These were always of a dramatic kind; sometimes the boys pretended to be on a train with John as the guard waving the flag or sometimes he would say 'I'm a shark' and pretend to splash about. He continued to look bored and uninterested in directed sessions and seemed to dislike class activities. He preferred watching other children do actions or would gaze around aimlessly, appearing self-absorbed.

During the final week's observation John's behaviour was similar in that his activities were centred on the same group of boys and he mainly rode around on tricycles, or climbed on the boxes. He continued to play with Andrew and they always wore their helmets during free play sessions. Directed sessions now seemed more enjoyable for John. He joined in songs with gusto and had learned the words and actions. He seemed fairly aggressive in defending his own or his group's territory. They had taken to sitting in a row on the bed for directed sessions and John would attempt to prevent other boys from sitting with them or trying to get on to the bed when there were no spaces left. He had extended his contacts among the children and, apart from the older boys, favoured two of the younger boys who had started nursery at the same time as himself. John's mother continued to bring him to nursery and take an active interest as far as possible in the things that went on. John had told her about the record sessions and she sent him with his favourite record to be played for the class. He enjoyed the occasion very much. Twice his mother arrived early at the nursery and stayed to wait for a lift for them to go home. He did not react to her presence apart from saying 'hello' and continued to play while she chatted with teacher. In the final week he also did a painting and drew an egg for Easter, the latter at the teacher's instigation as all the children were required to produce an egg picture.

Summary

John therefore had a distress-free entry into nursery and although at first he seemed self-absorbed in his private world, he slowly learned that to include others in his games he would also have to participate in theirs. His relationships with others were restricted to a small group of older boys in the first instance but gradually broadened to include a few others. He tended to ignore all girls and rarely approached staff members. John seems to typify the 'child relater' group, identified in the last chapter on the basis of statistical analysis.

At home his mother said he had been tired when he first started but this had worn off as the weeks went by. He now went to bed earlier than before and there had been few difficulties except those connected with his tiredness. She found him a strain during the first weeks as he seemed to do things that he knew would annoy her, like being destructive with toys, which he had not done before. By the time of the return interview, he was behaving quite well at home and was talking about going to the infant school. John's mother was preparing him by talking about school and explaining that it was for all day and that he would have dinner there as well. She felt he had been ready for the experience of nursery and that he would be better prepared for all-day separation and school than if he had been unable to go. His activities at home still included puzzles, games and stories. He had also cooked a sponge with mother's help and this had been eaten for tea, 'It tasted quite nice and he was so pleased with it'. Because his home life gave a fairly rich variety of activities, it probably did not matter quite so much that at nursery his self-directed activities were so restricted, since for John the major benefit of nursery attendance was his enjoyment of the company of other boys and learning cooperative play.

Emma

Background

Emma lived on the outskirts of the catchment area for the nursery in a small privately-owned terraced house. She had lived here for a year with her mother, who was divorced, and with her mother's friend and his five-year-old daughter. The adults' relationship appeared stable and they intended to marry as soon as convenient, particularly since Emma's mother was expecting a child. Each weekend the girls visited their other parents. Emma therefore went for the weekend to her father and his new wife. She also saw her grandparents on both sides on regular weekly visits. There were few young children nearby but Emma played with her 'sister' before the latter went to infant school and after she came home and occasionally with the boy next door who was younger than her. She was said to get on very well with her 'sister'. They played with dolls and watched television together; with the boy next door she shared toys cooperatively and specially liked his cars.

Emma's mother had a favourable attitude towards the nursery for the social benefits and play opportunities she believed it offered:

> She needs other children to play with. She seems bored and always waiting for Sally to come home from school. They have more animals and toys for them to play with at the nursery and can play with more messy stuff than they can at home.

Emma's mother felt that by two-and-a-half-years-old children were becoming more sociable and could actually play with another child as opposed to sitting next to them while playing on their own. She also believed that a child's learning ability was 'better' when they were younger – that, at this age, they had 'more capacity' for learning. She would have liked Emma to start at a nursery or playgroup by the age of two and a half but due to family circumstances this had not been a practical proposition and on entering nursery she was three-years-and-eight-months-old. Emma and her mother had visited the nursery, and the child had apparently enjoyed it and had not wanted to leave. She thought that Emma, while looking forward to the nursery, might be a little upset on the first day and intended to stay a little while until Emma got used to it, though she would not stay every day.

Entry into the nursery

1st day

Emma looks apprehensive and unhappy on entering the nursery with her mother but is not crying. Teacher-in-charge takes her to find a coat peg, saying, 'There, that's yours, right by the window, shall we take your coat off? In you go then and Mummy can stay as long as you like,' Emma slowly walks towards the nursery tables with the teacher who then turns back to mother saying, 'Come in, make yourself at home'. Emma's mother moves to stand near the Wendy House and watches while the teacher takes Emma around the nursery. She looks uncomfortable and out of place, and after going to the sand tray to say goodbye to Emma she leaves the nursery.

During the first morning Emma was introduced to the nursery routine. She did not look up for a few seconds when the music played for registration and when she did notice something new was occurring she stood and watched the other children make their way to the corner. A nursery nurse went to her and explained, 'When the music plays you come out to here', and led her by the hand to the mat. She sat near an older girl who later showed her how to put her milk ring on the bottle. Emma showed signs of wanting to cooperate and attempted to join in the hymn that followed register but she had little idea of the words. The older girl who had helped her earlier took her hand after milk and led her to the sand. During rhymes she volunteered to act as a horse in enacting the nursery rhyme and seemed to be enjoying herself. She clapped herself for her part when this was over. She tried to join in the actions for other rhymes but was not very competent, nor did she seem to know many rhymes; she would mouth as best she could while watching the other children. The teacher encouraged the older girl to take charge of Emma and they were seen together often over the first and second days. But by the end of the first week this contact was not so frequent and Emma was usually on her own.

Emma attended regularly for the first five days and was then frequently absent for odd days. These breaks in continuity appeared to have an unsettling effect. After the first absence she was tearful all morning and stayed near one of the teachers (the same one who had spoken to her the first morning) and sought adult contact as often as possible. On the eighth day she cried as she came in but did not cling when her mother left. Her behaviour was described by the observer for this day and the next:

Day 8
10.16 Seeking attention. Approaches helper several times and turns to watch her even when some distance away. Wants her to stay at the Plasticine table with her but does not follow when helper moves to different activity.

10.52 Chooses tambourine again for orchestra. Rolling it from side to side instead of tapping it when the music session is nearly over. Teacher demonstrates for her. Looks bewildered.

Day 9
9.45 Emma finds her own name ring from the three milk rings left. Sits in the middle of the floor for register. Looks pleased when teacher says to fetch shoe bag (for PE) as she now has plimsolls and has been given a bag.

10.35 In the main hall (for PE). Sits on the floor, waiting. Has to be told to join in. Watched different adults in turn and not one consistently – as a result often doing the actions behind everyone else or missing them altogether. She looks vacant when she does join in and not very happy.

Emma was a very quiet girl and never looked very well. She frequently had red blotches around her mouth and looked as though she had, or was about to have, a cold. She seemed shy and diffident towards other children though if she caught sight of her 'sister' Sally in the main school her face would light up and she would try to catch her attention through the windows. During directed sessions she tried very hard to do what seemed required of her by the adults in the nursery and her behaviour seemed extremely conformist in that she clearly worried when unable to produce the correct response – for example when she did not have any plimsolls or a bag. Some other new children were also without plimsolls but Emma appeared not to realize this nor the fact that they were generally unworried by it. Her desire to please adults and seek their approval was noticed on many occasions. In this her behaviour differed clearly from John's; whereas John was socially interested in other children, Emma's primary social awareness was towards any adult. In contrast to John she was therefore more typical of the 'adult relater' group, identified in the last chapter. One striking example came when she sat at the drawing table with a few children. They made a number of approaches to her in turn, one giving her a piece of paper and another a pencil while chatting to her. Despite this attention, she turned away from the table and sought the nearest adult in order to show her drawing. The observer learned to keep further away from her than was necessary with other new children in order to avoid Emma becoming attached to her rather than one of the members of staff.

For our final week of observation Emma was away on the first day and arrived on the next looking pale and wan. At first it seemed that very little had changed in her behaviour since the start of term. She was often engaged in solitary play and still sought out adults for approval of her achievements. The adult contact-seeking had however diminished overall, possibly through lack of encouragement. This meant that, on the first day we saw her near the end of term, Emma seemed more isolated than before. Over the following three days however it became clear that her whole manner towards the nursery had improved – she was less diffident with other children – and it appeared probable that her most recent illness and absence had created a temporary setback. Over the last three days' observations she interacted with other children while climbing on the boxes and joined in animatedly with other large muscle activities. This was a major change since she had previously chosen stationary activities. Her increased confidence showed at milk time when she fetched her bottle and removed the label without waiting for adult direction. She was more at ease in directed sessions and seemed to enjoy them more; having learned some rhymes she was more definite when joining in with words and actions.

At home Emma's mother felt that the nursery had had a beneficial effect on her daughter. She now spoke more, was more forthcoming and often seemed 'cheekier' than before entry, though she still did as she was told. Emma's mother had been upset on the days that Emma cried and when it was apparent that she was not very happy about entering the nursery. Emma's mother thought that the upset on entry was due partly to the fact that the child was unused to the company of other children en masse and to the fact that Emma was rather frightened of boys whom she had found too boisterous at first. Emma was a timid and shy child so the experience of nursery must have been somewhat overwhelming.

Summary

Prior to entry, Emma's home life in terms of toy play had been fairly restricted to passive pursuits of dolly tending, television watching and being read to, and so the nursery facilities offered her a much greater variety of experiences than were readily available at home. Her mother, while having a favourable attitude toward educational learning (the father less so in that he thought it was not so necessary for girls), felt she had little experience or knowledge of young children's development apart from her own child and few ideas as to how best to foster her daughter's all round development. The child's peer interaction was largely restricted to playing with her older 'sister' and in addition she may have found the relationships of adults in the homes she visited, and in which she lived, confusing; among them all her mother's presence was a reliable and constant factor.

She settled more slowly into the nursery than the other children illustrated here and her absences due to illness are unlikely to have helped this transition. Her anxiety regarding her home life and her attempts to make sense of it, were indicated at the nursery by her frequent approaches to staff with news of her real father and her stepbrother. It seems possible that if her mother had stayed for longer periods her transition into the nursery might have been easier. This however would only have been possible if mother had been given a constructive activity or task to do, because it was obvious by her manner on the first two days that she felt out of place and on her own admission this led to her leaving the nursery before she really wanted to. Once Emma became used to the pattern of nursery routine and the daily separations from her mother, she was able to begin exploring her surroundings in an increasingly adventurous manner both physically and socially.

Discussion

These descriptions of children entering the same nursery at about the same age provide an account of four different types of adjustment. Children were variously orientated toward adults, children and solitary activity, and exhibited varying degrees of timidity or signs of obvious upset. It appeared that the various reactions of children could be illuminated by knowledge of what went before and what was currently occurring in the home environment.

Our observations suggest that parents and teachers could work more closely together in planning a programme of activity for the individual child; by this means the child's home activity pattern could be taken into account. Because each child responds distinctively it would be helpful for staff to compile their own notes, no matter how brief, during the course of nursery activity or soon after. Within a few weeks a pattern should emerge and main trends in behaviour could be identified. Individual approaches could then be worked out by staff. For example, Laura might have settled better if she had been put with a small group of girls and given directed activities which involved them all. John's social progress was satisfactory but he was hardly utilizing much in the way of nursery resources and could engage in large muscle activities at home. Emma's transition was the slowest and most distressed. Involving her mother more might have helped: it seems that she was not ready for nursery.

A child's transition from home to pre-school may be hindered or helped by the total home environment. Most parents have the interests of their children at heart but these interests and attitudes will not always reflect the interests and attitudes of the staff in the pre-school setting. The parent is concerned with one individual whilst the staff have to look after the interests of a number of children. Even so, attendance at nursery can have an effect on the attitude of parents, for example in the case of Neil's mother who did not really care one way or another before entry about whether he went. Staff could do much to channel the parents' involvement with their children into an active partnership within which the parent at home attempts to reinforce the learning going on at nursery. Parents can only do this if they are kept informed about the activities and development of their children while they are at nursery. Laura's mother specifically wanted more information and yet had not approached staff. Parents in this survey were generally reluctant to be seen to 'rock the boat', believing that interference would not be in the interest of their children. This finding was corroborated by a parallel study at the NFER, concerned with transition into infant school (Cleave, Jowett and Bate, 1982), as was the desire for more detailed information on the nursery staff's aims and methods (for example as with Laura's mother).

CHAPTER 6

Follow-up Interviews with Parents

Thirty mothers were interviewed towards the end of the term in which their children entered one of the two nurseries used for intensive observations, that is, approximately ten weeks after the child's entry. They had all been interviewed prior to entry and this second interview was to obtain their views on how the children had reacted at home towards their nursery experiences, whether behaviour or play activities had changed and what type of contact parents had had with the nursery during the first term. We also wished to gauge the mothers' own feelings about nursery attendance. A semi-structured interview was used to obtain comparable information from parents. The mothers' reactions to their children's entry into nursery and their subsequent contact with staff is dealt with in the first half of the chapter; the second half discusses the children's behaviour and development following entry as described by their parents.

1. Mothers

Pre-school care and education is generally advocated in terms of its benefits for the child. Critics of such services can also claim to have the child's welfare at heart when stressing the undesirable effects of early mother and child separation or the mother's duty towards her offspring in nourishing his physical, social and psychological well-being. Mothers who appear to show signs of wanting to break out of the role, perhaps by finding a childminder, may be criticized by other mothers. If a mother seems too anxious to get her child into a nursery, the staff may also criticize: 'She can't wait to get rid of her children'. Yet as we have shown earlier the mothers in our study said they put their own children's welfare first when considering the reasons for sending their child to pre-school and gave a very low priority to the possibility of having time to themselves for their own activities. Since many of our mothers were child-centred in this way, one question concerned how they reacted when their child went to nursery and whether, once they had adapted to a new routine, they looked for new activities such as employment.

Mothers' reactions to entry

Over a third of the mothers said they had felt badly upset on the first day. Three had children who cried on entering the nursery:

> I felt rotten, I didn't really want to leave her. I felt I was pushing her into something she didn't want to do. But she needed the company of other children. I felt like this whenever she cried for the first few weeks.

> He screamed for the first four days. They had to hang on to him. Then on the fifth day he waved 'bye bye' like a big boy. I wasn't surprised at him being upset, we are terribly close. I felt upset. They said I could stay but I knew what (he) was like and if I stayed he'd expect it every day. It wasn't going to be fair on him really.

> I felt terrible . . . like lost. I still do now and I know he's only over the road.

The nine other mothers had felt upset even though their children appeared happy to stay in the nursery:

> When I got home I wandered round completely lost, looking for jobs to do and watching the clock. I remember I'd given up smoking and I kept looking for a cigarette and there wasn't one. I've started again now.

> I felt terribly lost for a couple of weeks. I suppose it was because normally when they've started school I've had another one at home.

> I felt a bit sick really, it was quite funny. I felt like that a few days. It was her going in the *school*, not just to the playgroup, her growing up and all. It's made me lonely. Perhaps it would be all right if I had another one.

A few of these mothers appeared to be upset because their child acted contrary to their expectations by entering the nursery without a backward glance:

> He was as good as gold, I couldn't believe it. I stood at the window watching and he didn't take any notice of me. I was upset actually . . . that he just went in like that with no bother at all. (Teacher) saw I was a bit put out and said I could stay but there was no point really, he was all right.

> I thought he would be upset but he seemed to like going, he never cried or anything. I was surprised because he wasn't used to being with anybody else. I was upset about it really, it was as if he didn't care about me.

In addition to the twelve mothers who had felt emotionally upset a number of others reported being worried prior to and for some days after entry:

> I was very worried as to the outcome. What if he did cry? I felt a bit confused wondering how he was going to be and what to do if he cried.

For the first week or so I had doubts as to whether I was doing right for him. He didn't *have* to go and I felt a bit guilty as though I was pushing him there. But I'm glad now, he looks forward to it and loves going. I wouldn't stop him now.

I was worried that she'd be all right. That she'd make some friends or something. There's no kids round here for her to play with.

She didn't want me to go at first, she wanted me to stay. I stayed five minutes or so and said I'll be back after milk. She didn't cry. I had expected her to be a bit reluctant, she'd always been with me. I thought she would have clung a bit more but I'm glad she didn't. I felt a bit lonely those first days. I kept thinking about her, hoping she'd be all right, hoping she'd settle in.

Over half the mothers, interviewed the second time, admitted to experiencing various degrees of distress or anxiety as their children began nursery education. This contrasts with the 15 per cent (of those mothers with children entering one of the two nurseries) who thought they might be adversely affected when interviewed the first time prior to entry. In the overall sample of parents interviewed, 21 per cent had expected an adverse reaction (see Chapter 3). It seems probable therefore that mothers underestimate their own reactions to the transition of their child from home to pre-school, believing that they will feel much as usual provided their child enters the new situation happily and settles down quickly. In nearly all of the above cases the child had not previously attended any other pre-school provision prior to nursery entry and it is of interest to note that a number of mothers who said they did not feel unduly upset or worried when interviewed had already experienced sending their child to a playgroup or childminder or day nursery. They sometimes recalled however that on these earlier occasions they had felt somewhat upset:

It didn't make much difference to me. He was going to playgroup every-day anyway. I was relieved when he started nursery but I felt awful when I left him the first time at playgroup.

By the time he went to this nursery I was used to him going. When he started at the other school (private nursery) I left him screaming and I felt upset as well as guilty. It didn't seem right, they didn't encourage you to stay at all to give them time to settle down. If a child showed any signs of being upset they shooed you out quickly.

Staying in the nursery

The majority of mothers departed after helping their children with coats or shoes and seeing them safely into the nursery. They generally stayed five minutes at the most from the time of arrival at the door even though they were told prior to entry that they could stay if they wished. Proportionately more mothers entered the actual play area with their children in Nursery B. Here the mothers were met individually by the teacher in charge on the first day and were given a verbal reiteration that they could stay as long as they liked and requested not to leave without making sure their children knew they were going.

Mothers from both nurseries however seemed to feel that their prolonged presence would not be desirable from the staff's point of view: 'They said you could stay and watch but in a way I think you do a favour for teacher by going. You're more a hindrance than a help' (Nursery B). A mother who was familiar with the staff at the other nursery put it bluntly: 'I didn't stay. I think (a staff member) prefers you out the way so she can get on with things.' Another mother at the same nursery said: 'They didn't say I could stay but I went in with him anyway. I only stayed a few minutes. I felt they (the staff) would rather I just took him in and came away really.'

It became clearer during these second interviews that another reason why parents did not stay was that they believed it would have been undesirable for their children; their personal preference to stay was of secondary importance. For example, a few had experienced staying with their child at a playgroup and their view is summed up by one mother: 'I decided not to stay because of what happened before when I helped at the playgroup. She used to hang around me and didn't want to play with the other children.' The mother's decision not to stay can be seen as consistent with the primarily social reasons they gave for wanting to send their child to nursery, that is, to learn to mix and share and find friends of their own age. So that while some mothers did not stay because they felt they would be in the staff's way, others felt that their presence would inhibit their child's adjustment to the nursery.

We have few concrete observations which would throw light on whether the mothers' worries on their child's behalf were justified since so few stayed for any length of time in the nursery. Of the six children who showed the greatest distress on entry four had mothers who stayed for periods up to 20 minutes on the first day and decreasing times thereafter. These children settled into their new surroundings, began to explore and make contacts with children and adults much earlier than the two whose mothers did not stay. The latter children remained non-communicative and generally withdrawn well into the middle of the term. It is of course not possible to say whether these two would have been helped by their mothers' presence in the way that the other four distressed children appeared to be, nor whether these four would have settled relatively quickly if their mothers had not stayed at all. What may be said with more certainty is that a minority of children showed distress on entry while a substantial proportion of mothers departed hiding their own anxieties. In these circumstances it would perhaps be to the mothers' advantage if nursery staff made clear their expectation that mothers should stay if they possibly could over the first two or three days. This would help some of the *mothers* over the hurdle of separation from their children and also provide them with a clearer understanding of what goes on in the nursery. Staff on the whole did not make such an expectation explicit and indeed it seemed that they did not want parents to hang around for any length of time over an extended period. Parents are sensitive to the atmosphere generated by those in charge of their children and are willing to defer to staff once their children enter school.

An open invitation to stay for a while does not seem sufficient. This was given in one nursery and mothers did go into its play area. However when their children left their side and began to play the mothers seemed to be at a loss to know what to do and did not stay. It is embarrassing to stand around in any new situation with no one to speak to or with no distinct aim in mind. A little direction from those in charge might help to alleviate the mothers' embarrassment. Instead of a vague 'have a good look around' the staff might suggest they help some children with a puzzle or talk to those who are painting. Given a task to do the parent can begin to feel comfortable in the nursery and build up confidence that her child will also be happy to be there when she had gone.

Contacts with staff

The establishment of a parent-staff relationship can be of vital importance for the future attitudes of parent and child to education. The mothers expressed their general satisfaction with the nursery in terms of its facilities and with the way the staff handled their children. Only one thought that a particular teacher was 'off-putting' to the extent that she felt unable to ask her anything. The majority felt it was possible to question the staff either on arrival or departure and that they were always ready to talk. None of the parents had felt any need to make a special appointment for a chat and most had asked how their children were settling in over the first week and on occasions since. Evidently parents as well as staff (see Chapter 2) feel that informal contacts do away with the need for formal ones. The mothers had been reassured by the teachers and had been given information on whether their children were playing with other children, drinking their milk and generally settling down. Despite this satisfaction it became clear during the interviews that mothers gained a lot of their information about what went on in the nursery through their children. In this way some mothers – those with communicative children – were aware of the different stories their children heard, of the songs and rhymes they listened to or had learned, and of the different children with whom they played. If pressed for more detail on other aspects of the nursery system parents often floundered. For example one mother explained:

To be honest I don't know what they do there. I haven't asked yet and I couldn't compare it anyway because I don't know what nurseries usually do. I think they're doing numbers or have a writing book now to prepare them for the next school. They have open evenings for you to show your interest but we missed that – I couldn't get a baby sitter and we (husband and wife) wanted to go together. I suppose it's up to you to ask them.

This mother and the majority of others felt that the onus was on the parent to request information. This may mean that the parent will ask for information on familiar topics, such as their children's behaviour, but will not necessarily like to ask about the educational development of their child in the nursery if this is seen as the teacher's domain. Indeed many parents were uncertain as to how much the nursery was directed toward preparing children for school work as opposed to establishing them in school routine. Parents spoke of the nursery as getting the child 'ready' for, or 'prepared' for, 'real' school but were on the whole not clear how this was taking place apart from establishing regularity of attendance in the company of specific teachers and children.

Some parents, then, were confused about the nursery's role in education, that is, in the narrower sense of academic learning. We shall see below that parents were also confused over the part they themselves could play in educating their children.

The staff at both nurseries had provided opportunities for parents to visit them since the start of the term. At Nursery A parents were invited to an open evening to meet the staff. Less than a third did so. Those who went had gone primarily to 'show interest' and, particularly in the case of the two fathers who went alone, to meet the staff. One mother had found the visit very helpful. She had thought the children would be playing all day and had been surprised to find that they were beginning to write by tracing round the teacher's letters and numbers. She had learned about her son's social progress with other children and had been able to set the teacher's mind at rest over her son's hearing. Of the parents who had not gone to the open evening three had not known there had been one, while others thought that it had occurred too early in the term for there to be anything to discuss, or that it was mainly to meet the staff and this they had already done. A few mentioned baby sitting problems and others thought the evening was for parents with particular problems. These parents did not seem indifferent to their children's progress because a number had gone to the school on another evening to see a film about helping your own child learn to read – though this was not specifically intended for the nursery children – and others had gone to help make sandwiches for the nursery party and to watch a play. The majority of mothers said they would want to attend the next open evening since their children would by then have been at the school for a longer period.

At the other nursery over half the mothers had gone to a monthly open day and two had gone more than once. These mothers too had gone mainly to show their interest but had an added incentive of being able to see their child at work and as one mother put it 'see what they're doing at the moment'. They had not participated in activities but appeared to have sat and watched for a while. One mother went along, 'so he knows I'm interested in what he does'. Another mother indicated that she went once for her son's sake rather than to learn anything for herself: 'They (children) don't do a lot at that age, do they, but I suppose they like to show you'. The mothers who had not gone were again not indifferent towards their children's experience in the nursery but, on the whole, had not seen the purpose of going. One mother said: 'It was mainly for mothers to sit and watch. I'd prefer to go in the evening to see what the child had done or have a particular report on the individual child. I'm not much for watching them.' Another mother had also not relished standing around watching and was influenced by one of the mothers who had already been: 'I toyed with going and then spoke to one of the mums who said it was a waste of time – her daughter hadn't shown her anything and I thought (son) would be a bit like that so I didn't bother'. At Nursery A a notice had been prominently displayed half way through term asking for parent volunteers to help during the morning or afternoon session. Only one of the mothers spoken to a second time had actually gone in to help. She went a few times and then stopped going. This is what she said:

> I spent a couple of mornings up there with a group of children. We did paintings and puzzles and played in the sand. But he (son) didn't seem to like it. He said I don't want you to stay anymore. Whether it was because I was talking to the other children or not I don't know . . . jealous like. I'd seen the notice up and teacher said to come two afternoons. When he didn't like it she said best not to come. She hasn't asked me to come again.

Nearly all the mothers had seen the notice asking for help and a few had thought they might like to go but were uncertain what they would be expected to do or whether they had any skills to offer. Some had children still at home and had thought they would be unable to take these with them. This poor response to the nursery was in contrast to the 54 per cent of parents who originally said they would willingly help in the nurseries that their children were going to attend. One explanation of the difference between intention and actuality is that staff failed to explain the nature of the help they required and, in the case of the one mother volunteer above (and another observed in the classroom but not interviewed a second time) failed to provide suitable support, encouragement or reassurance when difficulties occurred. A further reason for staying out of the classroom has already been alluded to: parents thought that their presence during the early days of nursery attendance would prevent their children making the most of opportunities offered. It would seem that if staff want meaningful contact with parents outside school hours or parents to help during the day they must provide explanations and varied opportunities to parents and accept that these efforts on their part may exceed the expected rewards before parents are able to become involved in the educational process themselves.

Changes in mothers' activities

Since mothers were not in the nursery, what were they doing with the few hours while their children were at nursery? A small minority had a younger child still at home and nursery attendance had not made a substantial difference to their lives in terms of personal freedom. Four mothers had found a job, two having decided to search for employment after their child had settled into the nursery. One of these mothers worked outside the nursery hours and a relation living in the family home cared for her child. Without the nursery this mother said she would not have been able to take a job as the housework would have been too much to cope with. As it was she could complete the housework while the child was at nursery and not feel guilty about leaving her mother-in-law to supervise tea and play before bed time. Two mothers who had been in part-time work prior to entry continued to use a childminder for the balance of hours that they worked; even though they worked part-time the nursery session was not long enough. One of these mothers found that the nursery entry had made her life 'very hectic'. She had had to shorten her working day by half an hour in order to find time to fetch her daughter from the childminder and deliver her to the nursery. The other mother had initially faced opposition from her husband over nursery entry since this would entail a change of childminder to one who lived nearer the nursery and who was prepared to take him there and fetch him afterwards. The mother had overcome problems of adjustment by delaying the child's entry until he had settled with the new childminder.

Prior to entry mothers had viewed the nursery primarily in terms of its benefits for their children. During the follow-up it was found that (apart from the above mother and the two who worked full-time) they came to appreciate the few hours' respite even where another child was still at home. Two pregnant mothers found it much easier to attend hospital, doctors or clinics for their check-ups and find time for a short rest. That 'a woman's work is never done' sprang frequently to mind when listening to how the majority of mothers spent their time. They used the nursery session to shop and do their housework, now finding these tasks quicker and easier to manage. Their social contacts had generally not expanded but, where coffee with friends was a feature of their lives, they enjoyed the luxury of being able to entertain or go out without having the responsibility of a young child. One mother, still with a child under three at home, had expanded her voluntary activities with local mothers and toddlers, appreciating the time she could devote to one child. The only problem now was providing individual attention to the child at nursery. A number of mothers mentioned that coping better with the household chores enabled them to devote time to their children for play or walks or other activities during the time they were at home. The mothers working outside the homes in the evenings, mostly at cleaning jobs, continued to do so and, in company with the mothers not contemplating work, did not think they would look for a daytime job until their children entered full-time school. The general feeling was that the nursery session was far too short to accommodate a 'proper job'.

2. Children

One purpose of the follow-up talks with parents was to obtain information about the children's behaviour at home following their entry into nursery. The children's immediate reactions to the nursery itself have been discussed in Chapter 4 and to some extent in the previous section with regard to mothers' own reactions. The majority of children settled into the nursery without giving their parents cause for concern. The few showing great distress in the early days of nursery attendance might have been expected to be more difficult at home during these first days but this, as far as we know, was not the case. The distress signs of crying, withdrawal or clinging appeared to be fairly specifically related to the actual nursery and once away from the school the children reverted to their usual behaviour until the time came to go to school the next day.

Developments in children's behaviour over the term are now discussed under the headings: the early days, general behaviour, contacts outside the home and toy play, and activities with parents.

The early days

Mothers reported few difficulties in coping with their children at home following entry into nursery. One of the commonest reports was of the children's tiredness over the first few weeks. Mothers said their children were sometimes more irritable than usual due to this tiredness and some said that their children fell asleep at odd moments during the day even though they had long given up their morning or afternoon naps. One boy fell asleep during his lunch after coming home from the morning session and fell asleep again towards the late afternoon. This little boy was observed to be still having such a sleep towards the end of the first term but most mothers said that signs of tiredness began to wear off by the end of the second or third week. A few children were being put to bed earlier than previously and some had to be woken up in the mornings in time to get ready for school. That this was more of a problem for the children attending the morning sessions was supported by those parents who commented that it had occurred later on in the term when their children had changed from the afternoon to the morning session.

One mother mentioned bed-wetting incidents on the first two nights and three said their children had wet themselves in the nursery. However, not all of the children were entirely reliable at home before going to the nursery and mothers on the whole did not think the nursery had had an adverse effect on the matter of toilet training. In fact one mother said her son had persistently wet himself at home but that after a few weeks in the nursery this had ceased. One mother said her daughter had had a few nightmares some weeks after the start of term. These had been isolated incidents and a contributory cause seemed to have been the stray worms being collected in the nursery by one of the teachers. The nightmares had not occurred since then.

Parents found themselves having difficulty in explaining that school did not open at weekends to children not yet used to the routine. Some children had wanted to go to school on Saturdays and Sundays and also return after they had had their lunch when they attended mornings or go in the morning when they attended in the afternoons. Holiday breaks created similar difficulties and parents whose children had been reluctant starters in the first instance mentioned that their children appeared apprehensive on their first day back after a holiday, but that their reluctance did not last more than a few days.

General behaviour

By the end of term the majority of parents said that any early reluctance had given way to enthusiasm. The children looked forward to going to nursery and even though they generally understood the accepted hours of attendance, often asked if they could go at the weekend, or if they could stay all day and have their lunch at school like the older children. Mothers did not report any dramatic changes in their children's behaviour at home in the weeks following entry but frequent comments on particular aspects of behaviour indicated that changes had been and were still taking place.

First and foremost parents mentioned an increasing independence of behaviour which they associated with the children being away from the home and parents for a few hours a day. They felt their children were learning to take notice of other adults and children and in doing so were learning to assert themselves. The mothers generally felt that this was one of the 'good' features of nursery:

It's a good thing for children to get used to being on their own. It's a start to their own bit of independence . . . to when they will be at school all day. The teachers treat them more like adults and discipline them so they walk not run in the nursery. It's a good thing, it gives them a bit of respect for the teacher for when they go to school.

The children were learning to do things for themselves, particularly where their development was behind that of their peers:

> They (staff) make them more independent. He has to do things at the nursery like going to the toilet on his own and washing his hands after-wards. He's started dressing himself now and seems more grown up, more independent and not so babyish.

Parents were not quite so endeared to other kinds of behaviour which they saw as another facet of this growing independence:

> She's more obstinate. She'll say 'Mrs ... (teacher) tells me you shouldn't do that' and won't always take notice of what I want her to do.

> He gives me a bit of backchat. I have to repeat myself. He is trying it on a bit ... thinks he's a big boy now.

and a final example: 'She's a bit rude, only to be expected I suppose now she's growing up. She's obstinate and won't take no for an answer. They are finding their feet.'

A second type of change, mentioned by mothers, was that their children were learning to mix with other children and were more sociable. Four children who had not previously had a particular playmate, had now found friends near their homes. Seven children however were still relatively isolated, except for their family members, and only saw other children while at nursery. Three of the children who had had frequent contact with particular playmates, prior to nursery entry, now had less contact with them during the hours at home. This was mainly because they saw their friends at the nursery or had found another child they preferred at the nursery. The few extremely shy children would now approach others while out shopping with their mothers and all the children had grown in confidence according to their mothers' reports.

The majority of mothers stated a third change: their children were 'learning to share' through being at the nursery. To a large extent however such statements were based on the parents' belief of what they thought was occurring, and what they thought should occur in the nursery environment. Interestingly, learning to share at nursery was not necessarily accompanied by similar behaviour in the home. A substantial minority of mothers made comments like the following examples and reminiscent of those made by the mothers speaking of independence:

> He's got cheekier since he started. He was always a demanding child and he is more so now. He won't wait and wants everything at once.

> He's got a bit naughty. Wanting what *he* wants all the time. In the nursery he can, I suppose, pick up anything he wants when he wants more or less.

He wants (brother's) toys all the time and is a bit underhand about it. He sneaks into the room and touches the toys when he thinks I'm not looking.

At home children who quarrelled with siblings prior to entry continued to do so and, in a few cases, mothers thought the arguments had got worse as the child at nursery got older. It did not seem as though sharing by taking turns, which parents saw as something learned in the nursery, was transferring to the home. It is also possible that it was not occurring in the nursery. Perhaps what the children were learning there was that the nursery equipment was communal property to which they had the same rights as the other children. It is relatively painless to share what is not your own and observation showed that with many alternative toys in the nurseries it was rare for a child to have to wait long before the toy he wanted became available. Two mothers believed that the variety of equipment and apparent freedom of choice available in the nursery had contributed to their children becoming more selfish and showing less consideration for other people's property when at home. The comment made by one mother of an only child provides a clue to a broader explanation of such behaviour:

He started off coming home grumpy and naughty. He would do things as if on purpose to annoy me like being a little destructive with his toys. He didn't take much notice when he was told to do something. I think it was a case of teacher overruled me as far as he was concerned. This has worn off now and he behaves himself when he gets home as he did before.

Such behaviour, variously described by mothers as demanding, naughty, rude and cheeky, therefore coexisted with the earlier mentioned signs of increasing independence and self-control. The child appears to vacillate between the two. Perhaps the 'naughty' behaviours can be seen as the child's efforts to draw attention to himself; firstly, as a way of ensuring that his place in the family and in particular his relationship with mother is as important now as it was before he went to nursery and, secondly, as 'testing' behaviours, using the familiar home territory as a sounding board while coming to terms with increasing independence of action.

Lastly, on the matter of language, one mother attributed her son's clearer speech directly to the efforts of the speech therapist who helped him at the nursery. Another mother, whose daughter's articulation had been poor, thought that it was now much clearer. However the majority of mothers believed that their children's language was progressing as it would have done without attendance at the nursery. A number thought that the acquisition of new words was due to the television programmes their children watched. Rude words, like bad habits, they attributed to the nursery. One mother said her daughter had begun to stutter 'like her friend', but another said her son's stutter was diminishing and he now spoke with greater confidence. Only one of the mothers stated that her child was acquiring a better vocabulary due to attending nursery. The child in question was forward in her speech before going to nursery and was now bringing home long words which the mother knew were not used within the family. Sometimes children misheard or confused words heard in the nursery and mothers had difficulty in knowing what they meant. For example one child came home and said 'I'm going to be a manger' and her mother thought perhaps she meant she was going to be a donkey in the manger for the Christmas nativity play. Later the teacher explained that the little girl was going to be 'an angel' in the play.

Contacts outside the home and toy play

The questions on toy play and contacts outside the home were repeated during the follow-up talks. As with other features of the children's behaviour, the interpretation of changes occurring since the nursery entry can only be tentative because we do not know whether such changes would have occurred even if the children had not had the nursery experience. Even so, changes in contacts outside the home were more certainly due to nursery entry. For example half the children were taken less often to visit their parents' friends because mothers tended to go out for tea or coffee while their children were at nursery. Visits to relations had remained the same because these often occurred at weekends. Visits to shops had remained about the same but the children who had gone on large shopping expeditions with mothers now tended to go only to the local shops near the nurseries.

Mothers reported four marked changes in their children's toy activities. The reduction in one of these – push-pull type toy activities – seems more to do with the age and maturation of the child than to nursery attendance. Only a third of the children had previously played with such toys on a frequent basis; the rest, according to their mothers had, 'grown out of them'. By the time of the follow-up only two or three children were still playing with such toys. The influences contributing to the next two changes in frequency of activities were less clear cut. There was a dramatic reduction in time spent riding bicycles, pedal cars or similar toys which had formerly been a popular activity for the majority of children. The weather was good when the follow-up interviews were conducted and the children were able to play outside if they wanted, so this was not a factor. One child's bike had been stolen and another two bicycles had broken. The rest had simply stopped riding on their bikes so frequently. Both nurseries had provided ample opportunity for this type of activity and perhaps the children found this sufficient. A less dramatic decrease had occurred in building or construction type activities involving Lego, bricks or similar equipment. Previously 80 per cent of children had played at least once a week or more with such toys but following nursery entry only half the children continued to do so. As with bicycles there seemed to be no obvious explanation other than that the nursery provided adequate opportunities for the children (mainly boys, see Chapter 3) who liked playing with construction toys. We have seen in Chapter 4 that it was the girls who played more with these toys in the nursery, in contrast to the situation at home prior to entry. The greatest change at home after entry had occurred among the girls. While the three girls who had played often with Lego or similar toys continued to do so, over half those previously playing with this at least once a week no longer did so. There was a similar shift for the boys but the majority still played in this way two or more times a week.

A fourth activity to show a change was that of painting but in this case there was a fairly substantial increase; two-thirds of the children were using paint at home twice a week or more whereas prior to nursery entry 60 per cent of the children had not painted at all. Parents who had not previously bought paint or who had had unhappy experiences with it possibly now realized that if their children could manage it at school it might also be tried at home without disastrous consequences. Other than these four clear trends the general trend was for slightly less time in all the other activities listed (see Table 3.2), for example with puzzles and plasticine with which half of the children had formerly played. Small cars, dolls and soft toys, formerly very popular, were still only slightly less frequent playthings.

Activities with parents

Earlier on, in the section on 'mothers', it was suggested that, although the amount of time mothers could spend with their children was reduced, they appeared to be making the most of the time they had with their children. Except for those who had found work during the day, mothers said they spent a similar amount of time playing with their children. The major difference between before and after nursery entry was that parents appeared to be emphasizing educational activities more than before. The children themselves were showing an interest in numbers and many mothers said they played counting games. Some had bought toy clocks to help with learning numbers, or puzzles and other items with numbers displayed.

Many parents were helping their children with writing which usually involved mother or father writing a number or the child's name over which the child would then trace. One mother had been advised by a teacher to write in lower case letters for her son after she had started using capitals. Parents still tend to use the latter for children at the beginning, perhaps because the letters are larger and clearer and they believe these will be easier for the child to copy.

A majority of mothers expressed interest in their children beginning to learn to read and a minority asked the interviewer when the nursery would start this or whether they themselves could do so and if so what reading schemes to use. Such parents had noticed their children's increased interest in the printed word and were beginning to wonder whether the nursery provided sufficient stimulation in this respect. Two mothers commented:

I don't know what they do as regards reading and writing. If there is a group for reading they should put some children aside and not let them play with the toys all day. They should encourage them as children of that age find it really interesting to learn to read. I would like a run down on what they do. All I know is they read them stories.

The education should start early. (Daughter) is picking reading up in that book. She can copy letters very good for her age, she is a forward child anyway. It's a shame, they get bored if they're left to themselves. They start to get naughty then.

As we have already stated, parents interviewed prior to entry gave priority to social reasons when considering the value of nursery attendance for their children. After entry it seems that on the one hand contact with the nursery raises the level of parents' awareness that their children are developing rapidly and are capable of learning more in the academic sense of reading, writing and number than they previously thought, whilst on the other hand they are uncertain of the nursery's educational role and are themselves unsure about taking active steps to influence such learning. Parents were least worried about helping with counting and writing. Most appeared uncertain about reading.

We would emphasize that all parents expressed general satisfaction with the nurseries. Only five parents indicated dissatisfaction of a specific nature. This minority seemed relatively educationally aware compared with other mothers and were anxious that their children should do well in school. These mothers tended to see free play – where children are left to choose for themselves – as unproductive in terms of learning. Another mother said that there was 'a lack of constructive activity', meaning that her son never appeared to make anything he could bring home. This was a familiar comment from mothers whose children had attended playgroup prior to nursery. These parents had attached a level of importance to visible achievements such as the models, drawings and paintings that had arrived home after at least one session a week at playgroup. They missed this evidence of productivity now that their children were at nursery.

Without such evidence it must be difficult for a parent to keep abreast of a child's development and, if they so wish, to reinforce learning taking place in the nursery. One mother had more feedback than the rest. Her son's speech problems had resulted in a speech therapist visiting him weekly at the nursery. After each session the therapist sent home weekly notes on what the parents could help him with during the following week. She had also advised both parents not to put pressure on their son with regard to learning until his speech difficulty had been overcome. The mother appeared to take a more relaxed and philosophical view of her son's handicap than she had shown at the earlier interview where her impatience with him, and her critical comparisons of him with his brother, had been evident. She was very willing to cooperate with the nursery, and the therapist's advice was helping her understand the problem and make constructive efforts with her son.

Concluding summary

Mothers experienced greater levels of distress when their children entered nurseries than they had anticipated. But, on the whole, mothers and children had adapted to the nursery routine by approximately ten weeks after entry when the follow-up interviews took place. In the home, children's activity patterns had altered to some extent and they were showing more interest in painting, drawing, writing, numbers and reading. Lacking a matched sample of children not attending nurseries, we can only tentatively suggest that some behavioural changes were directly attributable to the nursery – for example increased interest in painting and writing; other changes such as the less frequent play with push or pull along toys (excepting toy cars) are more likely to be attributable to maturation of the children.

The nursery environment could also be seen as having an indirect influence on the children through their parents. Parents appeared to be generally more aware of their children's potential for grasping new ideas and were focussing to some extent on educational activities which they saw as of use for the next stage of the children's school lives. While parents expressed their satisfaction with the nurseries and staff this seemed to be a satisfaction based on relatively little informed knowledge apart from what they gleaned from their children.

Parents seemed confused over the part they could play in educating their children and generally lacked knowledge on how to help foster their children's reading or writing skills. Cleave, Jowett and Bate (1982) confirmed this finding, as well as parents' general reluctance to admit that they were helping with these skills, with regard to parents of children starting infant school. While our parents seemed willing enough to discuss all their activities involving their children with the researchers it seemed that they had not asked of staff the questions which might have helped their understanding of the nursery system and of the progress of their children. They had been fairly lukewarm in coming forward to help in the nurseries and a low proportion had attended open days or evenings. To some extent their attitude arose out of a lack of appreciation of what nurseries were for and this was not helped by the staff who seemed not to have communicated how they set out to achieve their aims or indeed what these aims were.

CHAPTER 7

Conclusions

For the most part attention in this report has been on entry into nursery classes and nursery schools with some attention also paid to entry into playgroups. Each chapter has focussed on one aspect of the process of transition. In Chapter 2 a general account of the field was given by drawing on information from the survey of nursery schools and classes and playgroups. Chapter 3 took up the parents' perspective, examining their views on, and knowledge about, pre-school provision and describing some aspects of the children's home experiences. The children of some of these parents were then studied during their first term in nursery class and the results were presented in Chapters 4 and 5. Chapter 6 returned to the parents' point of view, examining their impression of their children's progress, the nursery and their own lives after their children had attended nursery for a term.

In Chapter 1, we stated that by concentrating on transition into nursery schools and classes we could produce a more focussed account which would nevertheless highlight issues arising in other forms of transition in the pre-school years. In this chapter we therefore widen our perspective and discuss some of our conclusions on transition in the context of the pre-school scene.

Overview of provision

At a very general level our study confirms that pre-school provision is both uncoordinated and patchy and that transition is a relatively unplanned process. The situation is uncoordinated, as we described in Chapter 1, because of the range of settings – nursery classes and schools, playgroups, local authority nurseries, private nurseries, childminders – and because of the different ages of entry, provision of equipment, level of curriculum planning, and public bodies to which pre-schools are responsible. The situation is patchy because there are wide regional differences in the extent and type of provision; for example there are wide differences between local education authorities in the provision of nursery schools and classes and day nurseries, and there are also differences between areas in the level of play-group provision. Examination of the relevant statistics also shows that the forms of provision interact in the sense that, for example, areas which have most playgroups tend to have fewer day nurseries (DHSS Personal Social Services, Local Authority Statistics).

After examining the extent of provision for three- to four-year-olds the Pre-School Playgroups Association concluded that some 82 per cent of three- to four-year-old-children attended some form of pre-school and that: 'Any substantial increase in numbers either in state nursery provision or in playgroups would now inevitably lead to a reduction in the other, or to wasteful over-provision' (*PPA Facts and Figures*, 1977). However this is a rather simple interpretation of the statistics. One crucial point, for example, concerns *choice* of provision; overall provision may seem high but in many areas parents may not be able to obtain the type of provision that they believe will meet the needs of their child and themselves. In the study it was found that parents' choice seemed largely academic in the sense that they were opting for what was available; given a free choice the majority wanted their children to attend a nursery school or class prior to entering a first or infant school. Our findings show that parents do not equate one form of provision with another. They believe for example that while both playgroups and nurseries cater for a child's social needs the latter caters at a higher level for the child's educational needs.

Another point is that many of the children included in statistics on pre-school attendance are four-year-olds and some of those are rising fives. Provision for younger children is not so extensive (see Chapter 1). This raises an issue, of specific bearing on transition, concerning the age of entry into pre-school.

Age of entry

The bulk of parents interviewed thought that their children would benefit from contacting other children from a very early age. It is interesting that this view is reinforced by research into the value of early peer interaction. In a classic article, Freud and Dann (1951) studied six young children who had been separated from their parents during the Second World War and brought up together in concentration camps. The researchers were able to observe these children at close quarters after they had been brought to England and concluded that their attachment to each other was passionately strong and had largely ameliorated the otherwise terrible loss of their parents – or, indeed, any stable adult figure. In a similar way, Hartup (1977) has pointed to the therapeutic effect of peer interaction to socially isolated pre-schoolers. Rather less dramatically, Blatchford (1979) and Lewis and Rosenblum (1975) and a growing number of others have pointed out its value to early social and intellectual development. Blatchford observed in some depth the naturally occurring interaction between pairs of children aged between nine months and 25 months. Even at this young age, a number of interactive developments were noted. Children could engage in alternating and reciprocal exchanges that, by their second birthday, were becoming colourful, playful and relatively sophisticated. It was suggested that interaction with a social and intellectual equal was qualitatively different from any relationship with an older person; rather than being led by more socially sophisticated elders, other children of the same age were partners and this seemed to facilitate interpersonal discovery and competence.

In this context the age of entry into pre-school takes on some significance. At present children rarely enter nursery classes or schools under the age of three years and, in the areas studied in this report at least, this also applied to playgroups. Any benefits or enjoyment that children might get from peer interaction before that age must therefore come from informal contacts in homes. Having brothers and sisters in the home is obviously a factor here, though it does appear that interaction between children separated by as little as two years of age differs from that between same aged peers (Shatz and Gelman, 1973). Only children will of course not have this option and in some cases we have encountered they can live in an environment bereft of any peer company at all.

The role of the playgroup

On the whole, then, there is at present little provision, at least on a formal level, for what could be a valuable experience for children. What can be done? Mother and toddler groups are one solution though parents in our sample had not enjoyed their experience of them. It seemed that some mother and toddler groups had too many people and too little by way of appropriate play material to be conducive to child/child interaction.

It is clear from some parents' responses that they would like playgroups to take children at an earlier age than three – say at two-and-a-half years. This many playgroups are reluctant to do and indeed the PPA view (in keeping with the view associated with Bowlby – see Chapter 1) is that the first three years of a child's life are best spent at home in the company of mother (Leach, 1978). In a practical sense a lot will depend in any case on individual children. Some may be relatively more dependent and immature, whilst others may be quite able to benefit from contacts away from their parents. Even so it seems on the evidence we have that pre-schools could be more flexible about the age of entry. Many children who could greatly profit from contact with others are currently denied this opportunity.

Taking a broad view of the pre-school scene, and given that nursery education is unlikely to be given resources for expansion (indeed, at the time of writing, existing resources are once more under threat), we can pinpoint a special role for playgroups. If some degree of pre-school experience below the age of three is considered to be valuable for children (and for the reasons outlined above we feel it is) then, because of the generally closer involvement of parents in playgroups, they are ideally placed to cater for children at this earlier age when they are dependent on their parents and may need them around. We recognize that the wrath of some playgroup enthusiasts might be aroused, but we are suggesting that the policy of entering children at three is not in line with parents' desires - not selfish desires but ones relating to the social needs of their children.

There is another reason for the potentially special role of playgroups for the younger pre-schoolers. Some parents thought an advantage of playgroups was that they had more control over the number of sessions they would like their child to attend. Parents seemed to want more flexibility at the start of their child's pre-school life than that provided by nursery schools and classes which, as at later stages in school life, usually require attendance every day. Easing the child into pre-school by gradually building up attendance in any case makes sense as an organizational tactic, though many schools would find it inconvenient. The greater flexibility and parental choice on the whole provided by playgroups could make a distinctive contribution to the child's first steps into a more formal setting outside the home.

Having considered the general pre-school scene with the arising issues of age of entry and the role of playgroups, the following discussion centres on some of the main conclusions we draw from our study of children, staff and parents and the importance we give to each of these in the process of transition.

Behaviour on entry into the nurseries

Of the children studied at the two nurseries (Chapter 4), the majority did not show signs of distress on entry. The staff perceived the children as predominantly well disposed toward themselves and other children, and parents - while experiencing a higher level of personal anxiety than they had expected when their child entered nursery - were generally pleased with the way their children had settled in to the nursery environment. On the whole, staff considered that children were settled into nursery school/class and playgroup by three weeks, though there were limits to the formation of particular friendships and the extent of taking turns and sharing. The case studies in Chapter 5 indicated that some children at least will progressively orientate toward nursery activities in terms of particular friendships with perhaps one other child, and there seems little doubt that this can aid adjustment to a strange situation. The majority of children, though, did not seem to have such a relationship after entry. Not all children, of course, are ready for, or require, friendship with peers, but in general this might be gently encouraged to good effect.

Systematic observation of children enabled us to chart the child's behaviour over the first weeks and again towards the end of their first term. In Chapter 4 we assessed how children's contacts were distributed in free play toward play material, other children and adults. Overall, rather more time was spent in solitary activities than in parallel activities or interaction with other children. It was found that children spent more time over the first three and the ninth week contacting other children than adults, that this was likely to take place in small groups of three to five children, and that these trends became more prevalent over the course of their first term in the nursery. The most popular activity types were 'large muscle', constructive activities of a 'gross' and 'fine' nature, dramatic play, and just watching proceedings in the nursery. As for toys, the most popular overall were large outside toys and dough, sand and water.

The behaviour of newcomers to the nursery class/school in sessions directed by staff (story, register, etc.) was of special interest because they are more structured than free play, and place more demands on the child's concentration and control. They are likely to be the first taste the child will have of formal instructional sessions that will become a central part of his primary school life, and are likely to place the most contrary demands on the child to those he will have experienced before. Informal observations indicated to us the extent to which some children found difficult even the most fundamental responses in such relatively controlled situations, like realizing the group has a leader to whom attention is required. Results from systematic observations, reported in Chapter 4, showed that bewildered or 'lost' behaviour tended to decrease over the first weeks, yet, interestingly, this was accompanied by an increase in both appropriate and responsive behaviour and also inappropriate, unresponsive or disruptive behaviour. Adaptation to this, the situation most structured by staff requirements, can therefore be in terms of behaviour congruent but also incongruent with those requirements.

The nature of the session appeared to be significant. The encouragement of staff in story and its own inherent interest seemed to facilitate appropriate, attentive behaviour whilst behaviour in register became progressively more disruptive, seeming to reflect, after an inital period of awe, that children were becoming impatient with a situation that required so little of them. The development of competence in instructional settings – so crucial in later school life – therefore owes much to the particular demands of the particular setting, indicating how important the appropriate choice of setting is likely to be.

One intriguing topic which warrants investigation concerns the processes by which newcomers become assimilated into an established group of children. It was not possible to assess this directly in the present study but informal observation suggested that even when separation from their parents seemed resolved, and children appeared ready to explore the pre-school environment, they still faced a formidable task in adjusting to a group of children, with its rules, rituals and power structure. To the child it must have been like being in a room with only one door and not knowing where to go to find the key. Some efforts have been made to explore this process (e.g. Feldbaum *et al.*, 1980; Phillips, Shenker and Revitz, 1951) but there is much that we do not know, e.g. concerning to what extent assimilation depends on the newcomers' own efforts or that of the group, which children find it easier to assimilate and for what reasons and what factors maintain the solidarity of the group.

Differences in children's reactions to entry

Staff interviews and questionnaires revealed differences between the earliest reactions of individual children on entry. Amongst reactions they identified were: the withdrawn reaction, the converse tendency to be over-excited and, of course, those who seemed to show no reaction, though a delayed response, several days or weeks after entry, sometimes occurred.

In Chapter 4 we attempted to arrive at a more systematic account of different types of behaviour by classifying children into groups on the basis of statistical analysis and in terms of a wide range of variables taken from the observation study, the Child Adjustment Questionnaire and the test of conceptual ability. Four different groups were identified and helped to formalize the descriptions of children's behaviour that came from interviews with staff. The variables used in the analysis, and listed in Chapter 4, were a representative cross-section of a range of attributes relevant to children's behaviour on entry into pre-school and the list may be useful as the basis of a profile of children's entry behaviour, possibly in the form of a checklist completed at regular intervals.

Statistical analysis cannot but depend on information reduced to measures amenable to quantification. Valuable as such analyses can be, they inevitably lose something of the full range and texture of behaviour. There is perhaps no alternative but the use of ordinary language with which to fully describe behaviour and in Chapter 5 we attempted to provide a more vivid picture of entry into nursery class/school by four case studies. These studies were based on notes of the children's behaviour and interviews with the children's parents before entry and again several months after entry. This gave us a wider perspective on children's entry behaviour than is probably accessible to most staff. Parents' views on their children's entry were especially interesting – before entry, in terms of what light it threw on children's behaviour on entry, and after entry, in terms of the extent to which the child's behaviour had matched expectations and the way the child now behaved at home.

Entry behaviour and previous home experiences

One of our main aims was to ascertain the extent to which children's behaviour at nursery was related to their previous experiences (see Chapter 4). A range of analyses highlighted a number of associations. The most solid was that between a measure of the home as a learning environment (the HOME schedule) and a number of measures describing children's behaviour at nursery. That is, those children with the higher home environment scores, engaged in more interactions with other children and positive behaviour in directed sessions, but were found less often in solitary and unoccupied activities in free play, and negative and lost behaviour in directed sessions. As would be expected from previous work using the HOME schedule in the USA (see Chapter 1), higher scores were also associated with higher scores of conceptual ability.

Even bearing in mind the unresolved issue of causality in any measures of association (i.e. which of the related variables causes the other, and whether both are perhaps caused by a third, unknown variable), there is evidence here that three-year-old children begin their school life with certain styles of behaviour that are related to their previous experience and home environment. One must not exaggerate the ease with which such associations can be identified; our results showed tendencies in certain directions but were hardly systematic across all variables. One could not, for example, present to staff with any confidence a list of child behaviour types and associated home experiences to watch out for in newcomers. But one can stress the need for a sensitivity toward possible associations, and one can say, on the present evidence, that attempts to 'start from scratch' when children come into the nursery are rather short-sighted.

Staff strategies

In Chapter 2 we considered ways in which staff acquainted parents and children with pre-school settings. The most common method was an individual discussion with a head or teacher followed by a visit to the nursery. Playgroups were less likely to have visits from parents prior to entry.

It seems clear that some form of prior contact between parent and child on the one hand and nursery or playgroup on the other can contribute to a smooth transition from home into pre-school. Whatever the type of prior contact that takes place one key aim must be to enable parents to become involved in the child's school life from the outset. Another aim concerns the easing of any traumas to child and parent that might be attached to transition. Janis (1964) concluded on the basis of a study of one child's entry into nursery school that familiarity with the place she is to be left, and positive attachment to the person with whom she is to be left, will lessen the child's anxiety, and repeated exposure to both in the presence of the mother will best bring this about. But every pre-school must form its own views on what type of contact it prefers. The important thing is that parents and children become familiar with the pre-school, so that they can both come to view transition realistically and with ease. It is important to evaluate prior visits in these terms. On this note some nurseries arranged prior visits, even home visits, with little sense of what they hoped to achieve by them. They payed lip service to 'parental involvement' whilst doing little to actively encourage or communicate with parents once in the nursery. It is not difficult for parents to feel uncomfortable in such situations and feel little desire themselves to become involved. A vicious triangle is formed when staff then comment on 'how uninterested parents around here seem to be'.

Once the child entered pre-school, staff adopted various strategies to help children adjust. One of these was staggered entry and another was allowing mothers to stay until children were ready to be left on their own (see Chapter 2). One thing that struck us when considering the approaches in different settings was not so much their content as the way in which they seemed to have evolved in isolation from each other. In other words staff in different settings had reacted to circumstances with certain strategies but there was little evidence that these were devised in consultation with others. In fact some staff at nurseries complained of how isolated they felt, both from the attached primary school in the case of nursery classes, but also from staff in other nurseries. Staff can no doubt obtain books on pre-school work if they are so inclined but many would no doubt prefer a more fundamental exchange of ideas with those faced with a similar task in other nurseries. Many said how valuable had been the occasional gatherings of nursery people in their area. In view of the current recession and restricted public expenditure, these are links that might be forged by headteachers and staff themselves, rather than relying on inspiration at county level. Similarly, staff in playgroups would benefit from exchanging experiences among themselves as well as with nursery and primary school staff.

Adult-child contact

To return to the types of strategies adopted by staff with newcomers, one thing of a general nature does stand out. This concerns the relatively infrequent contacts between adults and children (see Chapter 4). This is now an established finding from other research on pre-school children (Tizard, Philps and Plewis, 1976) and older children (e.g. Boydell, 1974; Garner and Bing, 1973), and has lost some of its surprise. It reflects to a large extent the difficult task staff face in distributing their time equally and comprehensively to all the children in their charge. At nursery level however, and especially with newcomers, one might expect more contact. Our own informal observations of staff showed instances when they seemed happy to let children play together or alone, provided they seemed reasonably absorbed, rather than feeding themselves into the action. One main point is that this approach can be too responsive in the sense that staff tend to become involved in newcomers' behaviour only *in the event* of some obvious need instead of taking a more directive approach and thereby being in more control. It means that children are left to play alone or make contact predominantly through relatively low level activities (see Chapter 4).

Results found in the Oxford Pre-School Project (Bruner, 1980) showed that more elaborated play is enhanced by a rather different nursery regime; elaborated play was fostered with fewer children and the stable influence of staff in providing structured and challenging tasks with a clear goal and accessible means to that goal (see also Cooper, 1981). These are likely to be key elements in helping children settle productively. No doubt children settle if left to their own devices – they learn in their way the 'rules' of the nursery and begin to act confidently – but this rather submits adaptation to the vagaries of good luck.

Research conducted by Barbara Tizard and her colleagues (1981) has shown, rather surprisingly in view of the popular notion that nursery schools can 'compensate' for conversational and learning inadequacies at home, that when adult–child conversations in home and pre-school are compared, it is in the former that one finds more complex and structured language use involving the child. This finding should encourage pause for thought, even if it is taken into consideration that staff have responsibility for more children and have to cope with other demands as well. It calls into question just what the aims of nursery staff might be, and, more specifically, what steps might be taken to enhance adjustment. Once again we do not wish to exaggerate the point. We recognize from our own observations, visits and questionnaires that many staff have sound ideas and a wealth of experience. But we have been led to wonder, as 'outsiders' considering the information before us, just how deliberately some have considered their aims and practice. Clarification might occur if staff felt bound to provide information to parents on their aims and methods of settling children.

Another useful policy would be the careful observation by staff of each child in turn in order to be clear about their behaviour on entry: what activities and toys they contact, how much contact they have with other children and adults and of what type. We have already mentioned a list of possible criteria that might be used (from the cluster analysis in Chapter 4). On the basis of profiles like this, brought up to date at periodic intervals, staff should be well placed to know how children are settling and what they might be directed towards.

Parents' views

A very important aspect of early transition is the knowledge held by, and differences in the attitudes of, people in the different settings. What information do parents have about nursery classes and school or playgroups? What information do staff in pre-schools have and request from other pre-school staff? Given that we are considering the practical case of a child moving from one setting to another, the information held by 'sending' and 'receiving' settings is highly relevant to continuity.

It was clearly seen from interviews with parents of two-and-a-half-year-olds (Chapter 3) that information held about pre-school settings arose principally through word of mouth. The bulk of information was channelled through neighbours, friends and relations and to a much lesser extent through official channels like government departments or from clinics or doctors. This is not in itself worrying but there are a number of possible drawbacks. One is that it tends to leave stranded those people who for one reason or another are not involved in a social network through which they would hear about local pre-school provision. Another cause for concern is that information passed by word of mouth can be partial and affected by personal and perhaps unfavourable experience. We would not wish to undermine the informal channelling of information – indeed a number of sociological studies (e.g. Young and Willmott, 1957) have shown its importance to the stability of a community. What appears to be required, though, is a clearer correspondence between formal and informal channels. Parents need to be aware of what pre-school facilities are available and which best serve their needs. For their part, agencies concerned in an official way with pre-school provision could well take a look at what parents actually think of, and know about, what they provide. They may well find, as we have, that parents have little idea which official body to approach in order to discover local provisions.

Nowhere is this more apparent than in the case of all day provision provided by day nurseries and childminders. There was a generally negative attitude toward these and the fact that parents were also generally uninformed about such settings surely carries a clear message to those who would like to improve their image. An unfortunate aspect about the present situation is that there is little need to 'sell' day nurseries and other settings because demand is so much greater than supply. This is no justification for complacency however because it can stabilize attitudes that strongly underlie divisions in pre-school care. For example, that parents view day nurseries so unfavourably can do little to foster the climate of cooperation and integration between 'caring' and 'educational' provision that so many people would like.

Parents' attitudes toward nursery schools and classes and playgroups were generally favourable. The vast majority of parents planned to send their child to one of these settings. A closer look at parents' attitudes toward these types of provision showed that the main value they saw to their child was social above all others. The greatest value was placed on learning to share and mix with other people. That more educational reasons for attendance are given a relatively lower priority should encourage some reflection about what such settings aim to provide. Obviously the social aim is high on anyone's list, but if staff aspire to foster the values of pre-school attendance for intellectual as well as social skills then there is cause for concern because this is not generally recognized by parents. Few government reports are better known than the Plowden Report (1967) but, even after its clear message about the value of play in learning, parents seemed to have little awareness of it as an issue, let alone the luxury of agreeing or not agreeing with it.

Lastly, on parents' reasons for desiring pre-school attendance, it was interesting to note how low a priority they gave to its value for their own benefit, for instance, to enable them to go out to work or to allow them time to do other things. It is possible that parents would feel guilty about admitting such things to an interviewer, though given the clearness of the trend it is difficult to imagine that such a suspicion has much foundation. Despite the benefits of pre-school attendance to children's parents, recently put forward by Hughes *et al.* (1980), parents in the present sample valued pre-school provision because of its benefits to the *child*, not to themselves. Cries from some people that nursery provision is required by parents for selfish reasons therefore seem unfounded. In any case 'benefits' to parents are necessarily limited when one considers that the bulk of children attend part-time sessions that last roughly two-and-a-half hours. This offers few possibilities for an extensive life away from their children even if parents should want it. The predominantly part-time form of pre-school provision, for example, is of little use to parents with a job; even full-day sessions at nursery school or class finish mid-afternoon and would probably have to be supplemented by other forms of child care. In addition, day nurseries will not usually take a child simply to allow parents to go out to work (places are normally allocated on the basis of need, for example, to the single parent).

Smooth transition: putting the three perspectives together

Our study underlines the close interdependence of the three parties to transition: children, staff and parents. Attention to only one or two perspectives will inevitably be only partially effective, and if one corner of the triangle is unhappily situated then the other corners will be potentially unstable. In the past most attention has been paid to children's behaviour. This is not to say that there is any necessary danger in doing no more, but transition would be enhanced if all three were involved and compatible.

Perhaps the most important general principle that can be stated concerning transition from one stage to another is that there needs to be continuity of environmental demands. That is, the demands of one stage must be compatible with those of the next. Several issues are involved here. In the first place the demands need not be the same. It is difficult to establish to what extent a new setting must differ before it inhibits or confuses children, or whether patterns of behaviour are set up that impede future adaptations. Certainly change and novelty are not in themselves necessarily a problem, even in the pre-school years. Indeed a child's learning and development largely depend on the confrontation between existing ways of understanding the world, inanimate or social, and new environmental demands. This is the essence of Piaget's theory of development, for example. Piagetians have discussed learning in terms of the most optimal discrepancy between cognitive structure and environmental demands. A rule of thumb seems to be that it must be different enough to stimulate the child's curiosity but not so dissimilar that the child becomes confused or frightened.

Applying this principle to transition from home to pre-school raises the issue of 'match' between the two settings. It is likely that the extent of 'match' will vary from child to child. Some parents may, for example, try to deliberately encourage learning of an 'academic' kind at home, and there is therefore likely to be a greater congruence of 'curriculum' in home and nursery class/school (though sometimes academic pressure at home can run counter to the culture of the nursery). 'Match' is also likely to be affected by factors associated with social class. It has often been argued that the values inherent in the school system and its language are essentially middle class in origin and that working class children therefore start at a disadvantage.

The special role that could be played by nursery education is to attend to discrepancies between the two settings prior to entry into formal schooling at five years of age. This is because the nursery setting is inevitably more child centred and informal and the circumstances of each child can be more flexibly dealt with. Children could then enter primary school with differences with their home environment already known and eased.

The two worlds of pre-school and home

The relationship between parents and pre-school staff following entry is crucial in the continuity of environmental demands, both because children will remain relatively dependent on their parents and because pre-school provision is predominantly part-time.

The results presented in this report are mainly based on the situation in two nursery classes, and generalizations must be cautiously derived. If the issues arising, however, are in any way typical – and it is our impression that they are – then a most important point concerns the lack of meaningful contacts between parents and nursery after entry. This does not show itself in a hostile attitude in either direction. Far from it. Parents and staff seemed generally satisfied with the child's progress once he had started. Rather, it shows itself in a more subtle way that became evident from interviews with parents after entry (Chapter 6) and observations in the nursery settings. All parents seemed to be interested in their child's life in the nursery but most, once they thought their child was coping, neither took, nor searched for, opportunities to obtain a more detailed account. Parents were generally wary of doing anything they believed teachers would find unacceptable and were fearful of being out of their depth with the more 'educational' demands. In consequence, they were interested but acquiescent and uninformed. Only a few expressed specific concern about certain things, such as what to do about helping their child read. For their part staff made some moves towards involving parents – for example, the notice requesting help in one of the nurseries – but did not articulate these moves very concisely and a direct appeal to parents on an individual basis might have been more fruitful.

Already, then, during the crucial first transition, one can see the child's two worlds slipping further apart. Alice Murton (1971) has stressed the need of a 'link' and not a 'break' between home and school. We observed something less dramatic that fell between these two extremes – more as if the two worlds were co-existing in 'parallel'. This can lead to missed opportunities; it means that a potentially valuable cooperation is not set in motion – one that would benefit the child, because he would expand his horizons by bringing aspects of the two environments in relation to each other, the parents, because they would gain confidence in and knowledge of their child's life away from home, and pre-school staff because experiences they consider important will then be communicated to those who care for the child in his home.

The onus seems inevitably to be on nursery staff to set the wheels in motion. Persistent and *explicit* attempts to let parents know how their child is getting on are required. We interviewed too many parents who had no more insight into their child's behaviour at nursery other than a vague impression like 'she's all right' or 'she enjoys it'. This is not to say that many staff do not make efforts and we recognize that the time available to them is limited. We also know that there are limits to what anyone can do if parents themselves are uninterested. Our point is that in the absence of consistent efforts, the two worlds will slip apart imperceptively through lack of meaningful exchange. This may be more comfortable for staff and parents in the short term but it is not in the longer term interests of either.

Nursery school/class and playgroup

We end with a comment about the transition pattern: home to playgroup to nursery class/nursery school. The relationship between playgroup and nursery is an important one and there is much that could be done to foster understanding and cooperation. Schools often had little by way of information on children coming to them from playgroups. Indeed some staff were hazy on what previous pre-school experience children had had. Some playgroup staff would have liked a lot more contact with schools, especially those into which they fed children. From the point of view of the child this exchange of information seems essential because, as we have shown elsewhere, it is important for staff to be able to set the child's current behaviour in the context of what went before. Suggestions were made earlier concerning visits by playgroup staff to schools and vice versa. All such suggestions are surely valuable for as we said in Chapter 2 the important thing to recognize is that both private and state run pre-school provision are likely to co-exist for some time to come and the more each understands about the role and contribution of the other, the healthier and less divided will be pre-school provision in this country.

APPENDIX 1

Results of Statistical Tests

Chapter 2 (Table 2.11) Differences between nursery and playgroup staffs' reasons for desiring pre-school attendance

Reason	2-tailed t-tests for independent samples
1) Enabling mothers to understand their children	t 1.87, p = 0.063 (203 df)
2) Enabling a child to learn through play	t −0.65, p = 0.515 (213 df)
3) Preparation for later school life	t −0.98, p = 0.328 (213 df)
4) Enabling a child to contact other adults	t 1.58, p = 0.115 (211 df)
5) Enabling a child to talk and listen and develop intellectual skills	t 2.62, p = 0.009 (212 df)
6) Enabling a child to develop coordination, balance and other skills	t 0.89, p = 0.373 (211 df)
7) Enabling a child to contact other children	t −1.75, p = 0.082 (211 df)
8) Enabling a child to be more independent	t 0.16, p = 0.869 (212 df)
9) Enabling mothers to have more time to themselves and their own activities	t −3.36, p = 0.001 (212 df)
10) Enabling a child to become part of a group	t −1.62, p = 0.106 (211 df)
11) Enabling mothers to meet and get advice from staff	t 1.7, p = 0.091 (210 df)
12) Enabling a child to engage in activities he couldn't easily do at home, e.g. messy play or use of apparatus like climbing frames	t −3.09, p = 0.002 (213 df)
13) Enabling the child to learn how to share and behave with other children	t −1.6, p = 0.12 (213 df)
14) Enabling mothers to make friends with other mothers	t −3.95, p = 0.000 (213 df)
15) Enabling a child to gain a lasting educational advantage	t 2.68, p = 0.008 (203 df)

Chapter 3

(1) χ 13.37 (2 df) p > 0.005
(2) χ 10.3 (2 df) p > 0.01
(3) χ 11.64 (2 df) p > 0.005
(4) χ 7.84 (2 df) p > 0.05

Chapter 3 (Table 3.7): **Differences between parents' and nursery and playgroup staffs' reasons for desiring pre-school attendance (2-tailed t-tests for independent samples, p < 0.05)**

Reason	Parents *v.* playgroup staff	Parents *v.* nursery school/ class staff
1) Enabling mothers to understand their children	t −3.65, p<0.001 (147 df)	t 6.37, p<0.001 (216 df)
2) Enabling a child to learn through play	t −2.78, p<0.01 (153 df)	t 2.7, p<0.01 (226 df)
3) Preparation for later school life		t −2.58, p<0.02 (225 df)
4) Enabling a child to contact other adults	t −2.26, p<0.05 (152 df)	t 4.29, p<0.001 (225 df)
5) Enabling a child to talk and listen and develop intellectual skills		t 4.3, p<0.001 (225 df)
6) Enabling a child to develop coordination, balance and other physical skills	t −3.32, p=0.001 (151 df)	t 5.26, p<0.001 (224 df)
7) Enabling a child to contact other children	t −2.34, p<0.05 (151 df)	
8) Enabling a child to be more independent	t −3.32, p=0.001 (150 df)	t 4.1, p<0.001 (224 df)
9) Enabling mothers to have more time to themselves and their own activities		t −2.65, p<0.01 (225 df)
10) Enabling a child to become part of a group	t −2.31, p<0.05 (152 df)	
11) Enabling mothers to meet and get advice from staff		t 2.59, p=0.01 (223 df)
12) Enabling a child to engage in activities he couldn't easily do at home, e.g. messy play or use of apparatus like climbing frames	t −3.26, p=0.001 (152 df)	
13) Enabling a child to learn how to share and behave with other children	t −2.22, p<0.05 (152 df)	
14) Enabling mothers to make friends with other mothers	t −4.86, p<0.001 (153 df)	
15) Enabling a child to gain a lasting educational advantage		

Chapter 4

(1)   Differences between Nursery A and Nursery B on the observation data significant in only one case: total adult/child contacts – t 3.53, p = 0.001 with 49 df.

4.2   *General results from the Observation Schedules, and Child Adjustment Questionnaire*

Comparisons between the frequency of behavioural categories over all four weeks performed by two-tailed t-tests for correlated samples. n = 51 and 50 df for all tests.

(2)	Solitary *v* parallel activities	t 2.38, p < 0.05
(3)	Solitary *v* child/child interaction	t 1.71, p < 0.1
(4)	Small groups *v* pairs	t 5.98, p < 0.001
(5)	Small groups *v* large groups	t 21.16, p < 0.001
(6)	Child/child interaction *v* total adult/child contact	t 3.68, p = 0.001
(7)	Adult child 'disciplinary' contacts	
	v 'Educational' contacts	t 4.2, p < 0.001
	v 'Help' contacts	t 5.37, p < 0.001
	v 'Managerial' contacts	t 6.14, p < 0.001
	v 'Together' contacts	t 4.95, p < 0.001
(8)	Amount of contact with teachers	
	v nursery nurses	t 2.7, p = 0.01
teachers	*v* other adults	t 9.27, p < 0.001
	v mothers	t 10.43, p < 0.001
	v students	t 10.64, p < 0.001
Nursery nurses	*v* other adults	t 7.28, p < 0.001
	v mothers	t 8.56, p < 0.001
	v students	t 7.19, p < 0.001

4.3   *Changes in behaviour in the nursery during the first term*

Differences between weeks were assessed by one-way repeated measures analyses of variance. Scores for the first, second, third and ninth week (W1, W2, W3, W9) were then compared in pairs at a time by two-tailed t-tests for correlated samples.

(9)   Differences between weeks in amount of solitary activity were significant – F (3, 132) 9.29, p < 0.001. T-test results. W1 *v* W2: t 2.75, p < 0.001; W1 *v* W3: t 2.57, p < 0.05; W1 *v* W9: t 5.65, p < 0.001; W2 *v* W9: t 2.32, p < 0.05; W3 *v* W9: t 3.04, p < 0.01.

(10) Differences between weeks in parallel activity were significant - F (3, 132) 2.62, p < 0.05. T-test results. W1 *v* W9: t 2.21, p < 0.05; W2 *v* W9: t 2.54, p < 0.05.

(11) Total adult/child contact. F (3, 132) 2.13, p < 0.1. T-test results. W1 *v* W9: t 2.39, p < 0.05; W3 *v* W9: t 2.21, p < 0.05.

(12) Differences between weeks in child/child interaction were significant - F (3, 132) 9.29, p < 0.001. T-test results. W1 *v* W2: t −2.35, p < 0.05; W1 *v* W3: −2.95, p < 0.01; W1 *v* W9: t −6.25, p < 0.001; W2 *v* W9: t −4.73, p < 0.001; W3 *v* W9: −4.72, p < 0.001.

(13) Differences between weeks in frequency of small groups were significant - F (3, 132) 3.09, p < 0.05. T-test results. W1 *v* W2: t −2.27, p < 0.05; W1 *v* W9: t −2.75, p < 0.01.

(14) Differences between weeks in frequency of large groups were significant - F (3, 132) 3.27, p < 0.05. T-test results. W1 *v* W3: t −2.04, p < 0.05; W1 *v* W9: t −3.34, p < 0.01.

(15) Child/child vocalizations. T-test results. W1 *v* W9: t −6.27, p < 0.001; W2 *v* W9: −4.88, p < 0.001; W3 *v* W9: −4.8, p < 0.001.

(16) Adult to child vocalizations. T-test results. W1 *v* W9: t 3.16, p < 0.005; W2 *v* W9: t 2.7, p = 0.01; W3 *v* W9: t 2.44, p < 0.05.
Child to adult vocalizations. T-test results. W1 *v* W9: t 2.2, p < 0.05; W2 *v* W9: t 2.12, p < 0.05; W3 *v* W9: t 2.83, p < 0.01.

(17) There were significant differences between weeks in 'Purposeful Movement' - F (3, 132) 8.94, p < 0.001. T-test results. W1 *v* W2: t 2.33, p < 0.05; W1 *v* W3: t 4.53, p < 0.001; W1 *v* W9: t 5.71, p < 0.001.

(18) Differences between weeks in 'positive' behaviour in story were significant - F 5.88, p < 0.001.

(19) Differences between weeks in 'negative' behaviour in register were significant - F 3.68, p < 0.01.

(20) Differences between weeks in 'lost' behaviour in register and story were significant - F 8.28, p < 0.001; F 7.19, p < 0.001 respectively.

4.5 *Associations between Parental Interview Data and behaviour after entry*

(21) Total HOME score and child/child interaction: r = .51, p < 0.01
and 'constructive gross': r = .33, p < 0.05
and 'unoccupied': r = − .32, p < 0.05
and 'solitary': r = − .52, p < 0.01.

(22) Total HOME score, and 'positive' and 'lost' behaviour in directed sessions: r = .47, p < 0.01; r = − .62, p < 0.001 respectively.

(23) Total HOME score, and total McCarthy score and 'verbal' subscore r = .38, p < 0.05; r = .38, p < 0.05 respectively. (Correlations involving 'perceptual' and 'quantitative' sub-components were not significant at the five per cent level.)

(24) Differences between girls and boys in the amount of 'art' and 'constructive fine' activities. $F (1, 31) 5.33, p < 0.05$; $F (1, 31) 3.87, p < 0.06$ respectively.

(25) Difference between girls and boys in their attitude toward teachers χ 10.45 (2 df), $p < 0.01$.

(26) Difference between girls and boys in 'negative' behaviour in directed sessions $F (1, 31) 5.45, p < 0.05$.

(27) Difference between first born children and second, third, fourth and fifth born in the amount of 'watch', 'unoccupied', 'solitary' and 'dramatic' activity: $F (1, 31) 4.79, p < 0.05$; $F (1, 31) 4.26, p < 0.05$; $F (1, 31) 5.15, p < 0.05$; $F (1, 31) 4.6, p < 0.05$ respectively.

(28) Difference between only children and those with siblings in the amount of 'dramatic' activity: $F (2, 30) 3.44, p < 0.05$.

(29) Difference in the amount of 'dramatic' activity, child/child interaction and solitary activity between children whose mothers spent under one hour playing with their children per day and those who spent over one hour. $F (1, 31) 4.07, p < 0.05$; $F (1, 31) 4.14, p = 0.05$; $F (1, 31) 3.59, p = 0.07$.

(30) Difference in the extent to which children took turns (Child Adjustment Questionnaire measure) between those with prior pre-school experience and those without it: $\chi 6.06$ (2 df) $p < 0.05$.

Coding Form for Free Play Session

CHILD _____ DATE _____ OBS. SHEET _____ TIME _____

MIN	ACTIVITY Watch, Un., Wait, Cr., P.M., Con. F., Con. G., Non-C., 3Rs, Art, Lg. mus., Dom., Dram., G. Rule, Inf. G, SNP	Toy type	Solitary	Voc. to self	CHILD/CHILD				ADULT/CHILD			Identity T NN O.Ad Moth. Stud.	Emotion Distr. Aggr. P'tive Lost Neutral	Position Ins. Outs.
					Social part level Par. Int.	Size of group Pair S.Grp Lg.Grp	Child action Init. Resp. Tog.	Vocaliza-tion Ch. O.Ch Tog. N. Verb.	Adult type of cont. Educ. Help Manag. Soc. Discip.	Child action Init. Resp. Tog.	Vocaliza-tion Ad. Ch. Tog.			
1														
2														

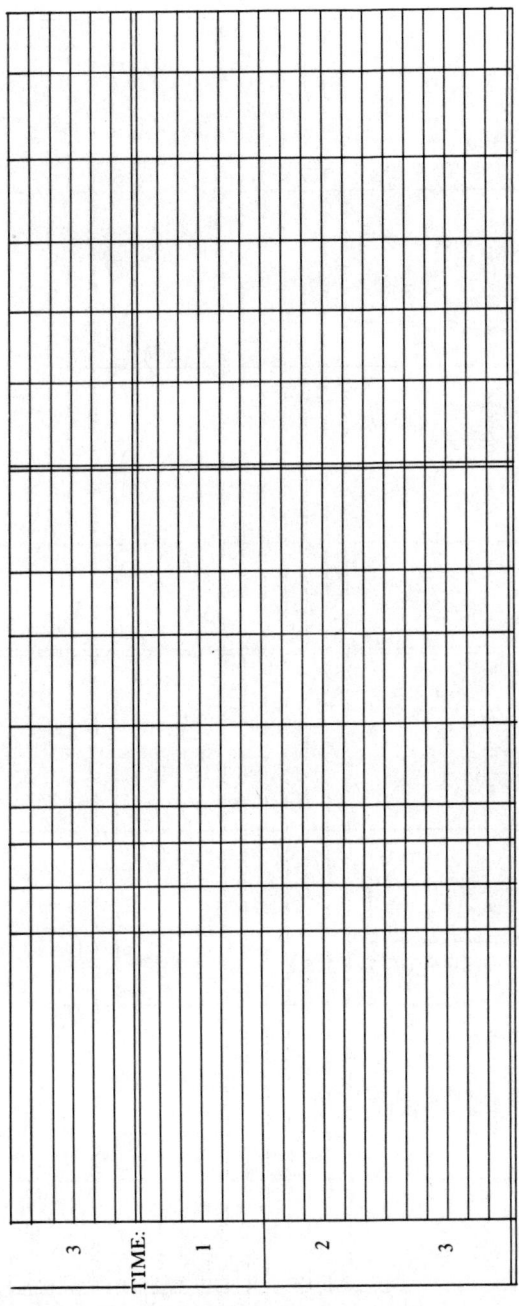

Directed Sessions Coding Form

	SESSION Register Milk Story Rhymes/Songs Music	BEHAVIOUR (Attn. required) 1) Attend 2) R. App. 3) R. Inapp. 4) In. spont. 5) Lost 6) Int. 7) Move away 8) Domestic	BEHAVIOUR (Attn. not required) 9) App. 10) Inapp. 11) Lost		SESSION Register Milk Story Rhymes/Songs Music	BEHAVIOUR (Attn. required) 1) Attend 2) R. App. 3) R. Inapp. 4) In. spont. 5) Lost 6) Int. 7) Move away 8) Domestic	BEHAVIOUR (Attn. not required) 9) App. 10) Inapp. 11) Lost
Date Time 1 —				Date Time 7 —			
Date Time 2 —				Date Time 8 —			
Date Time 3 —				Date Time 9 —			

Date								
Time								
4——								
Date								
Time								
5——								
Date								
Time								
6——								
Date								
Time								
10——								
Date								
Time								
11——								
Date								
Time								
12——								

APPENDIX 4

Inter-observer Agreement: Free Play and Directed Session Categories

The formula used to calculate inter-observer agreement was:

$$\frac{\text{No. of agreements} \times 100}{\text{No. of agreements and disagreements}}$$

Figures are based on simultaneous coding in the nursery situation by two observers.

Free play

Categories not listed below did not occur during the reliability study.

Activity[1]	88.9%
Toy type	97.2%
Solitary	81%
Voc. to self	63.6%
Child/child social participation (parallel and interaction)	81.8%
Size of group	94.6%
Child action (initiation)	63%
Vocalization (target child voc. and together)	63.2%
Adult identity	66.7%
Emotion	91.9%
Overall agreement figure	84.4%

---

[1] Analysis of observer agreement was usually based on behaviours taken together within a subsection, e.g. the 'activity' categories (large muscle, constructive gross, etc.) were taken together, as were toy type, size of group, etc. The reason for this was because of the low frequencies of some behaviours within a subset, and for convenience in calculations.

Directed sessions

'Lost' and 'move away' were not coded during reliability study. For the other categories (i.e. those that combined to produce 'positive' and 'negative'), observer agreement figures were 87.5 per cent before combination (i.e. agreement based on each category taken individually) and 93.8 per cent after combination. In other words, disagreements over categorization were ironed out to some extent as a result of combination.

Bibliography

AINSWORTH, M. D. S. and WITTIG, B. A. (1969). 'Attachment and exploratory behaviour of one-year-olds in a strange situation'. In: FOSS, B. M. (Ed) *Determinants of Infant Behaviour*, Vol. 4. London: Methuen.

ANASTASI, A. (1966). *Psychological Testing* (Second edition). New York: Collier-Macmillan.

ARRINGTON, R. E. (1943). 'Time sampling in studies of social behaviour: a critical review of techniques and results with research suggestions', *Psychological Bulletin*, 40, 2, 81-124.

BAUM, L. (1953). The adjustment of the newcomer to the nursery school. Unpublished report. University of London Institute of Education.

BLATCHFORD, P. (1979). The development of social interaction between infants. PhD thesis. University of Surrey.

BLATCHFORD, P. (1982). Children's Entry into Nursery Class. Unpublished paper.

BLURTON JONES, N. (1972). (Ed) *Ethological Studies of Child Behaviour*. London: Cambridge University Press.

BONE, M. (1977). *Pre-School Children and their need for Day Care*. London: HMSO.

BOWLBY, J. (1965). *Child Care and the Growth of Love* (Second edition) (First edition published 1953). Harmondsworth: Penguin.

BOWLBY, J. (1971). *Attachment: Attachment and Loss*. Vol. 1. Harmondsworth: Penguin.

BOYDELL, D. (1974). 'Teacher-pupil contact in junior classrooms', *British Journal of Educational Psychology*, 44, 3, 313-18.

BRADLEY, R. H. and CALDWELL, B. M. (1976). 'Early home environment and changes in mental test performance in children from 6 to 36 months', *Developmental Psychology*, 12, 2, 93-7.

BRUNER, J. S. (1980). *Under Five in Britain*. London: Grant McIntyre.

CASLER, L. (1961). 'Maternal deprivation: a critical review of the literature', *Monographs of the Society for Research in Child Development*, 26, 2 (whole no. 80). no. 80).

CHAZAN, M., LAING, A., COX, T., JACKSON, S. and LLOYD, G. (1976). *Deprivation and School Progress. Studies of Infant School Children*. Volume 1. Oxford: Blackwell.

CLARKE, A. M. and CLARKE, A. D. B. (1976). *Early Experience: Myth and Evidence*. London: Open Books.

CLARKE-STEWART, K. A. (1973). 'Interactions between mothers and their young children: characteristics and consequences', *Monographs of the Society for Research in Child Development*, Serial No. 153, 38, 6-7, Dec.

CLEAVE, S., JOWETT, S. and BATE, M. (1982). .... *And so to School: a Study of Continuity from Pre-School to Infant School*. Windsor: NFER-Nelson.

CLIFT, P., CLEAVE, S. and GRIFFIN, M. (1980). *The Aims, Role and Deployment of Staff in the Nursery*. Windsor: NFER-Nelson.

COOPER, M. G. (1979). 'Verbal interaction in nursery schools', *British Journal of Educational Psychology*, 49, 214-25.

CURTIS, A. and BLATCHFORD, P. (1981). *Meeting the Needs of Socially Handicapped Children: The Background to My World*. Windsor: NFER-Nelson.

CURTIS, A. and HILL, S. (1978). *My World*. Windsor: NFER.

CYSTER, R., CLIFT, P. and BATTLE, S. (1980). *Parental Involvement in Primary Schools*. Windsor: NFER.

DAVIE, R., BUTLER, N. and GOLDSTEIN, H. (1972). *From Birth to Seven*. London: Longman.

ELARDO, R., BRADLEY, R. and CALDWELL, B. M. (1977). 'A longitudinal study of the relation to infants' home environments to language development at age three', *Child Development*, 38, 595-603.

ENDSLEY, R. C., HUTCHERSON, M. A., GARNER, A. P. and MARTIN, M. J. (1979). 'Interrelationships among selected maternal behaviours, authoritarianism, and preschool children's verbal and non-verbal curiosity', *Child Development*, 50, 331-9.

FELDBAUM, C. L., CHRISTENSON, T. E. and O'NEAL, E. C. (1980). 'An observational study of the assimilation of the newcomer to the pre-school', *Child Development*, 51, 497-507.

FREUD, A. and DANN, S. (1951). 'An experiment in group upbringing'. In: EISSLER, R., FREUD, A., HARTMANN, H. and KRIS, E. (Eds) *The Psychoanalytic Study of the Child*. Volume 6. New York: Int. Univ. Press.

GARNER, J. and BING, M. (1973). 'Inequalities of teacher-pupil contacts,' *British Journal of Educational Psychology*, 43, 234-43.

GARVEY, C. (1977). *Play*. London: Fontana/Open Books.

GREAT BRITAIN. DEPARTMENT OF EDUCATION AND SCIENCE. CENTRAL ADVISORY COUNCIL FOR EDUCATION (ENGLAND) (1967). *Children and their Primary Schools*. Plowden Report. London: HMSO.

HARTUP, W. W. (1977). 'Peers, play, and pathology: a new look at the social behaviour of children', *Newsletter* (Fall) Society for Research in Child Development.

HUGHES, M., MAYALL, B., MOSS, P., PERRY, J., PETRIE, P. and PINKERTON, G. (1980). *Nurseries Now*. Harmondsworth: Penguin.

JANIS, M. G. (1964). *A two-year-old goes to Nursery School: A case study of Separation Reactions*. London: Tavistock.

LEACH, P. (1978). 'What shall we do with the under-threes?' *Contact*, January.

LEWIS, M. and ROSENBLUM, L. (Eds) (1975). *Friendship and Peer Relations*. New York: Wiley.

LEWIS, M., YOUNG, G., BROOKS, J. and MICHALSON, L. (1975). 'The beginning of friendship'. In: LEWIS, M. and ROSENBLUM, L. (Eds) *Friendship and Peer Relations. The Origins of Behaviour, Volume 4*. New York: Wiley.

LIEBERMAN, A. F. (1977). 'Preschoolers' competence with a peer: relations with attachment and peer experience', *Child Development*, 48, 1277–87.

McGREW, W. C. (1972). 'Aspects of social development in nursery school children with emphasis on introduction to the group'. In: BLURTON JONES, N. (Ed) *Ethological Studies of Child Behaviour*. London: Cambridge University Press.

MAY, O. E. (1963). *Children in the Nursery School: Studies of Personal Adjustment in Early Childhood*. London: University of London Press.

MUELLER, E. and LUCAS, T. (1975). 'A developmental analysis of peer interaction among toddlers'. In: LEWIS, M. and ROSENBLUM, L. A. (Eds) *Friendship and Peer Relations. The Origins of Behaviour, Volume 4*. New York: Wiley.

MURTON, A. (1971). *From Home to School*. Basingstoke: Schools Council/Macmillan.

NEWSON, J. and NEWSON, E. (1975). 'Intersubjectivity and the transmission of culture: on the social origins of symbolic functioning', *Bulletin of the British Psychological Society*, 28, 437–46.

PALMER, R. (1971). *Starting School: A Study in Policies*. London: University of London.

PHILLIPS, C. J., WILSON, H. and HERBERT, G. W. (1972). A study of inadequate families. Child Development Study (Birmingham 1968–71).

PHILLIPS, E. L., SHENKER, S. and REVITZ, P. (1951). 'The assimilation of the new child into the group', *Psychiatry*, 14, 319–25.

RENWICK, M. (1978). Going to School. Paper presented to NZ/OECD Conference on early childhood, care and education, Massey University.

RHEINGOLD, H. L. (1969). 'The effect of a strange environment on the behaviour of infants'. In: FOSS, B. M. (Ed) *Determinants of Infant Behaviour, Volume 4*. London: Methuen.

RUTTER, M. (1972). *Maternal Deprivation Reassessed*. Harmondsworth: Penguin.

SCHAFFER, H. R. and EMERSON, P. E. (1964). 'The development of social attachments during infancy,' *Monographs of the Society for Research in Child Development*, 29, 3 (whole No. 94).

SHATZ, M. and GELMAN, P. (1973). 'The development of communication skills: modifications in the speech of young children as a function of listener', *Monographs of the Society for Research in Child Development*, 38, 152.

SHINMAN, S. (1975). Parental response to pre-school provision: a study of 77 families, focussing on the characteristics of those who chose not to use a new community playgroup. Unpublished report. Brunel University.

SMILANSKY, S. (1968). *The Effects of Sociodramatic Play on Disadvantaged Children: Pre-School Children*. New York: Wiley.

SMITH, P. and CONNOLLY, K. (1972). 'Patterns of play and social interaction in pre-school children.' In: BLURTON JONES, N. (Ed) *Ethological Studies of Child Behaviour*. London: Cambridge University Press.

SYLVA, K., ROY, C. and PAINTER, M. (1980). *Childwatching at Playgroup and Nursery School*. London: Grant McIntyre.

TIZARD, B. (1981). Language and social class in the pre-school years: Labov revisited. Paper given to the annual conference of the British Psychological Society, Guildford, Surrey.

TIZARD, B., PHILPS, J. and PLEWIS, I. (1976). 'Play in pre-school centres: play measures and their relation to age, sex and I.Q.', *Journal of Child Psychology and Psychiatry*, 17, 251–64.

TIZARD, B., MORTIMORE, J. and BURCHELL, B. (1981). *Involving Parents in Nursery and Infant Schools: a Source Book for Teachers*. London: Grant McIntyre.

TIZARD, J., MOSS, P. and PERRY, J. (1976). *All Our Children*. London: Temple Smith.

TOUGH, J. (1977). *The Development of Meaning*. London: George Allen and Unwin.

VAN DER EYKEN, W. (1977). *The Pre-School Years (Fourth Edition)*. Harmondsworth: Penguin.

WELLS, G. (1976). Language development in pre-school children. SSRC Report, University of Bristol.

WHITE, B. L. and WATTS, J. C. (1973). *Experience and Environment: Major Influences on the Development of the Young Child, Volume 1*. New Jersey: Prentice-Hall.

WHITE, B. L., KABAN, B. T. and ATTANUCCI, J. S. (1979). *The Origins of Human Competence*. Farnborough: Lexington Books.

WOODHEAD, M. (1976). *An Experiment in Nursery Education*. Windsor: NFER.

WOOTTON, A. J. (1974). 'Talk in the homes of young children', *Sociology*, 8, 2, 277.

WRIGHT, H. (1966). 'Observational child study'. In: MUSSEN, P. H. (Ed) *Handbook of Research Methods in Child Development*. New York: Wiley.

YOUNG, M. and WILLMOTT, P. (1957). *Family and Kinship in East London*. Routledge and Kegan Paul.